Building UNIX®
System V Software

Building UNIX®
System V Software

Israel Silverberg
Uniware (Israel), Ltd.

P T R Prentice Hall
Englewood Cliffs, New Jersey 07632

Library of Congress Cataloging-in-Publication Data

Silverberg, Israel.
    Building UNIX System V Software / Israel Silverberg
        p. cm.
    Includes bibliographical references and index.
    ISBN 0-13-370008-9
    1. Operating systems (Computers) 2. UNIX System V (Computer file)
    3. Computer software-Development   I. Title.
QA76.76.063S5584 1994   93-24020
005.4'3--dc20   CIP

Editorial/production supervision and interior design: *Harriet Tellem*
Cover design: *Lundgren Graphics*
Cover photo: *Westlight*
Manufacturing buyer: *Alexis Heydt*
Acquisitions editor: *Gregory G. Doench*

©1994 by P T R Prentice Hall
Prentice-Hall, Inc.
A Paramount Communications Company
Englewood Cliffs, New Jersey 07632

The publisher offers discounts on this book when ordered in bulk quantities. For more information, contact: Corporate Sales Department, PTR Prentice Hall, 113 Sylvan Avenue, Englewood Cliffs, NJ 07632. Phone: 201-592-2863, Fax: 201-592-2249.

The author and publisher of this book have used their best efforts in preparing this book. These efforts include the research, development, and testing of the theories and programs to determine their effectiveness. The author and publisher make no warranty of any kind, expressed or implied, with regard to these programs or the documentation contained in this book. The author and publisher shall not be liable in any event for incidental or consequential damages in connection with, or arising out of, the furnishing, performance, or use of these programs.

UNIX is a registered trademark of UNIX System Laboratories, Inc. in the U.S. and other countries.

Printed in the United States of America
10 9 8 7 6 5 4 3 2 1

ISBN 0-13-370008-9

Prentice-Hall International (UK) Limited, *London*
Prentice-Hall of Australia Pty. Limited, *Sydney*
Prentice-Hall Canada Inc., *Toronto*
Prentice-Hall Hispanoamericana, S.A., *Mexico*
Prentice-Hall of India Private Limited, *New Delhi*
Prentice-Hall of Japan, Inc., *Tokyo*
Simon & Schuster Asia Pte. Ltd., *Singapore*
Editora Prentice-Hall do Brasil, Ltda., *Rio de Janeiro*

To my sister, Laila,
for the many years of support.

Contents

Preface

There is no question that the field of software engineering has been undergoing continual change. Not only have we seen change in the area of software tools, we have experienced change in our views of the software engineering process. In trying to develop zero-defect software, we have learned that the process is as important as the tools. The number of books written on this subject in the past few years reflects our concern with the process of software engineering. As expected, most of these books deal with the principles of software engineering. In this book we apply those principles to the building of software in the UNIX environment.

This book concentrates on one area of the software engineering process – the build process. This process deals with the transformation of a collection of source files to a software package. This transformation can be expressed in the following formula:

```
source files + tools + build instructions = software package
```

On the whole, this book is not concerned about the software tools used to build a software package. The primary emphasis is placed on build instructions, which describe how to apply the tools to the source files. The **make** command is the UNIX tool that executes the build instructions, which are contained in description files called makefiles. Chapters 3 through 6 show how to write makefiles. Yet, if we are to maintain control of the build process, we must also control the tools that transform the source files. Chapter 7 shows how to manage those software tools.

The remainder of the book deals with miscellaneous topics that often arise during the building of a software package. Chapter 8 looks at software package administration by covering software package maintenance and configuration. Chapter 9 shows how macro preprocessors can be used in the build process. Chapter 10 reviews how to use a series of tools that can modify an object module. Finally, in Chapter 11, the special problems that arise in the building of archive libraries and shared libraries are discussed.

In this book, we discuss the writing of build instructions and the control of software tools, but we do not discuss version management of source files. This topic was discussed in a previous work (Israel Silverberg, *Source File Management with SCCS*, Englewood Cliffs, N.J.: Prentice Hall, 1992). Although source file management and building software are separate disciplines, they do overlap. In those areas of overlap, I have attempted to provide sufficient information for this work to stand by itself without becoming a dissertation on source file management.

Yet, as much as we try to separate the different disciplines in software engineering, there must be an overall consistency to our chosen process methodology. Thus, this work and the work on source file management were written to reflect an integrated approach to software management. Both books are based on the existence of a software library and that all information necessary to build a software package exists in the SCCS source tree stored in that library. This means we can retrieve all the source files for a software package in one instruction, build the package with a second, and install it (or create a distribution media) with a third. This can happen with an integrated approach to source file management and building software.

When I wrote the first book, I left out the source code for all the makefiles because I did not want to discuss the problems of building software in a book on source file management. This book provides the missing files and a few changes needed to build the package as it evolves in this book. For those readers who do not have the first book, the makefiles described in this book can be still used as models for any software package.

In the end, I hope that this book sheds some light on the subject of building software in the UNIX environment.

Acknowledgments

As every writer knows, the development of a manuscript into a book involves many people who help in many different ways. For her unwavering support and help in reviewing the first drafts of this book, I wish to give special thanks to my wife, Haya. I also wish to thank Barbara McGrath who helped check the page proofs. Thanks to Greg Doench, my editor; and Harriet Tellem, the production editor for the book; for their work in bringing this book to life. Thank you to the many people whose names I do not know, including the reviewers of the book and the other members of the Prentice Hall staff, for making the publication of this book possible.

Israel Silverberg
Karmiel, Israel

Ordering Information

The example software shown in this book is available in computer-readable form. For ordering information write to:

Uniware (Israel) Ltd.

P.O. Box 11151

Karmiel 20100 Israel

You can send e-mail to:

silvrbrg@techunix.technion.ac.il

Text Conventions

Throughout this text, the following conventions will be used to illustrate UNIX commands.

- In example statements, any input that must be entered will be in **boldface**.

- Words that are enclosed by **braces**, { }, are command-line parameters and are to be replaced with the appropriate text.

- The presence of **brackets**, [ ], indicates that the enclosed text is optional. Multiple options are separated by a **vertical bar**, |.

- **Ellipses (...)** indicate that the preceding option may be repeated.

- Text enclosed in < > indicates variables whose content is determined by the command being executed.

- The Bourne shell will be used for all examples (C shell users should have no problems making the appropriate changes). The beginning of a shell command line is indicated by a **$**.

- All software has been tested under System V/386, Release 3.

CHAPTER 1

The Problem

1.1   Introduction

As the title suggests, this book is about a development task that must be faced in every software development project - building software. Yet, what does *building software* mean? We often associate building software with the transformation of a source file into a finished object. For example, a program source file must be processed by various tools such as a preprocessor and a compiler to create an object module. Even a shell script may be passed through a preprocessor so as to include common routines or to incorporate commands for different machines. In both cases the raw materials (source files) must be transformed into a finished component (executable files, data files, libraries, and the like).

Building software refers not only to the building of a single component, but to the building of the total set of components related to a single application. To make the application ready for use, we must also include other maintenance and configuration components. Although the AT&T documentation uses the term **software package** slightly differently,[1] it is used here to refer to the entire set of components that make up a single application. Since it is possible to have components that are not part of the software package, the components that make up the software package are called **package objects**. These package objects can be divided into three categories, as defined next.

Every software package has one or more package objects that form the reason for the existence of the package (whether it is a C compiler or a General Ledger package). These objects are called the **application package objects**. As with all package objects,

---

[1]These terms are similar to those used in AT&T, *UNIX SYSTEM V RELEASE 4, Programmer's Guide: System Services and Application Packaging Tools* (Englewood Cliffs, N.J.: Prentice Hall, 1990), p. 8-2. However, we use the term package object to reference all files that are included in the software package, whereas, in the cited work, the definition excludes packaging files.

there is no distinction between executable object modules, shell scripts, libraries, or data files. Even the name of a directory is considered a package object.

Besides application package objects, a software package may include other sets of objects. One such optional set contains the package objects used to install and remove a software package from a system. We call this set of package objects the **maintenance package objects**. As we shall see, whether the software package is installed on one machine or many, the need for these objects remains the same.

Once a product has been installed, it may need to be configured to the particular environment in which it is to be used. For example, a communication's software package may require that we define a default serial port. The package objects that perform this configuration function are called **configuration package objects**. Many software packages mistakenly combine the configuration package objects with application package objects. Later in this chapter, we shall discuss why the two sets of objects are distinct and must be treated separately.

From the previous discussion, we see that *building a software package* refers to the transformation of source files into application package objects, maintenance package objects, and configuration package objects. In this book, we will not be concerned with how source files are transformed. Instead, we will concern ourselves with the transformation process or, in other words, the **build process**. In this chapter, we examine the general principles of the build process. In Chapter 2, we present an overview of the UNIX solution, which will then be discussed in detail in the remainder of this book.

As the first step in the review of general principles, we need to analyze the build process. We then are ready to discuss the structure of the source tree and its relationship to the building of a software package. And finally, we look in more detail at maintenance package objects and configuration package objects and how they fit into the picture. All this is combined and shown in an example software package. This example software package will then be used throughout the book as the basis for the building of a software package.

1.2   The Build Process

The transformation of the source files for a software package into package objects is known as the **build process**. This build process can be described by the model shown in Figure 1.1. In some organizations, the build process may be called *building a product*. However, the word product implies something to be sold, and what we are discussing applies to all software.

This build process can be accomplished by manually executing each step required to build the product or by using a set of tools designed for that purpose. The following section discusses the characteristics of the build process, whether manual or automated. From these characteristics, we can proceed to define the requirements for the build process.

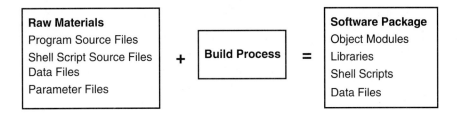

Figure 1.1 The Build Process

1.2.1 Characteristics of the Build Process

The build process occurs not once but many times throughout the life of a software package. This repetition appears in a series of distinct but overlapping cycles as follows:

1. *Development cycle:* Since human beings tend to make occasional mistakes, we must repeat the "develop - verify" cycle until the software package meets the design specifications. Each time we repeat the cycle, we repeat the build process.

2. *Software assurance cycle:* After the development group finishes with the software package, it then goes through, or should go through, a product assurance group. This group verifies that the product can be built according to the instructions provided and that it does, in fact, comply with the design specifications. Depending on the defects found by the product assurance group, the software package may be sent back to the development group. As the software package cycles between the development cycle and the product assurance cycle, the build process is repeated at least once if not several times.

3. *Software version cycle:* Some software packages may be a one-time affair, but most will go through many revisions during their life. Whether it is a result of fixing problems or the addition of new features, the software package will have cycles 1 and 2 repeated many times.

1.2.2 Requirements of the Build Process

From the preceding, we can see that the build process must be able to produce the same results repeatedly. In other words, given the same set of source files, the same tools, and the same build instructions, the same software package should be produced. As obvious as this process may seem, it is a major obstacle in software development. To better understand why this is a stumbling block, let's go back over the elements in building a software package in more detail.

1. *Source files:* That to produce the same output depends on having the same input seems like a self-evident requirement. Unless only comments are changed, any change in a source file (the raw materials of the build process) will result in building a different package object.

2. *Tools:* The tools (that is, a compiler or a macro preprocessor) are the active transformation agents in the build process. Just as many tools may be used to build a wooden table, the transformation of one or more source files into a package object may require one tool or several tools. For example, the compiling of a C program may require the use of a macro preprocessor, the C compiler, an optimizer, and a link loader. On the other hand, a shell script may only pass through a macro preprocessor. In either case, changing versions of the tools used in building a software package may alter the final product.

The term **tool** refers not only to the executable module that transforms the file, but also to the ancillary files that are part of the tool. For example, the object library files and standard include files must be controlled for they also influence the final product.

3. *Build instructions:* **Build instructions** describe how a product is to be built. With properly documented instructions, the same source files and the same tools will result in the same software package. When the instructions are changed or are incomplete, the results of the build process may not be the same. Therefore, the ability to successfully build the same software package given the same source files and the same tools means that we must be able to control how it is built.

Build instructions can be divided into two categories. The first category contains the options and arguments to the tools. While not always true, changing an option or an argument may alter the package object. For example, the **-f** option (use floating point emulation) of **cc** may have a significant effect on the resultant object module. On the other hand, the **-H** option (print pathname of files used on *stderr*) will not affect the object module.

The second category of build instructions defines the tools to be used and their order of execution. Such an instruction may require that only source files that have changed be processed. This instruction would reduce verification requirements because package objects that have not changed since the last time they were verified need not be verified again.

As we can see, for the build process to be repeatable, the following must be done:

The same source files must be processed by the same tools with the same build instructions to produce the same software package.

This statement seems obvious. Yet violation of one or more of the elements of this simple statement remains a constant problem in software development. Why? We could give a long and complicated answer. Instead, in sum, these requirements are details that are not considered important to a creative person. In fact, the task often incurs a certain amount of disdain because it is not considered part of the "real" effort in software development. However, in the past few years, we have begun to grasp the importance of the process of software development. While the above statement is very simple, it does encapsulate the process for building a software package. In this work, we shall look at how to control what software tools are used for and how to write build instructions. How to manage source files was discussed in a previous work.[2]

1.3   Structure of the Source Tree

In this section, we briefly review the relationship between the structure of a source tree and the build process. Those readers who are experienced software developers may wish to skip this section.

A software package consists of one or more package objects. Each package object, in turn, is the result of the transformation of one or more source files. In this work, the term **component** is synonymous with package object. Occasionally, a package object (component) may result from the combining of one or more **subcomponents**. We define the component, and occasionally the subcomponent, as the smallest unit of a product that can be built. Figure 1.2 shows the source file structure for the hypothetical software package.

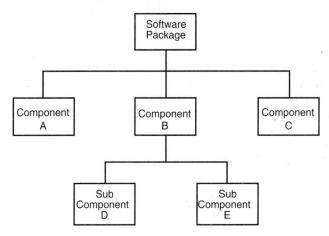

Figure 1.2 Structure of Hypothetical Software Package

---

[2]For more information on source file management, see Israel Silverberg, *Source File Management with SCCS* (Englewood Cliffs, N.J.: Prentice Hall, 1992).

From the preceding discussion, one could get the impression that components are independent units. This may not be the case. It is possible for components to have interdependent relationships. For example, one component could be an object library (see Chapter 11 for more details). This object library may be both a package object and a component used to build other components. It may also be used only for the building of other components and not be a package object. Thus, we can expand our previous statement to say that package objects are a subset of the total number of components used to build a software package.

The structure of the hypothetical software package can be translated into practice by defining a directory for the package and subdirectories for each component and subcomponent. By adding the source files to this hierarchical structure, we have a **source tree** (see Figure 1.3 for an example).

The source tree exists in two different forms. When the source files are in the source library under the control of SCCS, we call this an **SCCS source tree**. The machine on which the SCCS source tree resides is called the **source library machine**. When retrieved from a source library, the source files become part of the **work source tree** that is used for development of the next version. While the SCCS source tree and the work source tree may be on the same machine, we still define the work source tree as residing on the **development machine**.

From the days when the source library machine and the development machine were the same, the work source tree often existed as subdirectories to the SCCS source tree. Whether the machines are the same or not, this practice should be stopped. The maintenance of source file security and integrity requires that the work source tree always be created under a different root directory than the SCCS source tree.

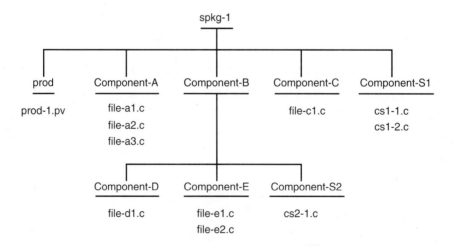

Figure 1.3 Source Tree for a Hypothetical Software Package

The **product version file** (prod-1.pv in Figure 1.2), while not used to build the software package, bonds the work source tree with the SCCS source tree. SCCS supports the tracking of the version history of individual source files source but ignores the version of the software package. Therefore, the product version file tracks the version history for the entire software package. The tools that manage the product version file were described in another work.[3]

In summary, by structuring the source tree as a series of components, we provide an organized structure for the building of a product. At the lowest level, we can build subcomponents from their source files. Components can then be built from subcomponents or from source files. Finally, by combining all the components that are package objects, we can build a software package. Just as we build a program from discrete units called functions or modules, we can build a software package by using the same technique.

1.4   Maintenance Package Objects

What does installation of a software package have to do with building a software package? Before we can answer this question, we must understand what the term installation means within the context of a software package.

Just as we do not build a software package in the source library, we do not build it in the verification or target directories. Instead, we retrieve the source files for a software package from the SCCS source tree and place them into a work source tree that is outside the domain of the source library. When we build the software package, we direct the output of the build process to a **package image tree**. This package image tree will always be a mirror image of the target directory structure in which the software package will be used. For example, if a software package was installed in /usr/spkg-1/bin and /usr/spkg-1/lib, then the package image tree would be {image directory}/spkg-1/bin and {image directory}/spkg-1/lib.

After successfully building a software package, the package objects must then be transferred to either the verification machine or the target machine. For a moment, let's assume that the development machine, verification machine, and target machine are all the same physical machine. Under this condition, the package image tree would then be transferred to a **verification path** for verification of the software package. For example, the preceding software package would be transferred to {verification directory}/spkg-1/bin and {verification directory}/spkg-1/lib. Once the software package has cleared the verification phase, it would then be transferred to the **target path**.

However, we do not transfer software packages; we install them. We can therefore define **installation** as *the process of transferring a software package from the development machine to the verification or target machine*. Besides the transferring of package objects from one machine to another, the installation process may execute the necessary housekeeping routines needed to make the software package usable.

---

[3]These tools are discussed in Silverberg, *Source File Management with SCCS*, Chapter 11.

Although we stipulated that all this takes place on one computer, such may not be the case. The source library could be on one machine, the **source library machine**; the product could be built on a second machine, the **development machine**; verified on a third machine, the **verification machine**; and placed into use on yet another machine, the **target machine**. Under these conditions, the installation process requires moving the package image tree to an intermediate **installation media** (for example, a floppy disk or a tape) and then to the verification machine or the target machine.

The installation process forms one part of the maintenance package objects. The other part is the set of package objects that can remove a software package from the verification machine or the target machine. If done properly, the removal process will leave the machine in the same state as it was prior to the installation of the software package.

Other than forming another component in the software package source tree, why discuss package maintenance? Unless the package objects are placed directly in the verification path or the target path, a software package must be installed to be useful. Also, an organization should have one standard for installing software packages. Therefore, if these objects must be a part of every software package, then it is appropriate that they be discussed as part of an overall discussion of building software packages.

1.5   Configuration Package Objects

Installation is the first step in getting a software package ready for use. In addition, many software packages must be configured to operate within the environment of a particular system (for example, communication ports or printer types). The maintenance of these parameters is part of the **package system configuration** functions. So as not to confuse these functions with the system administration functions of UNIX, we will refer to them simply as **package configuration**.

There is, or should be, a difference between the **maintenance package objects** and **configuration package objects**. However, one occasionally encounters a software package in which all the package configuration functions are embedded within package maintenance. This is a poor practice, since configuration parameters are subject to change after the package has been installed. They should, therefore, always be kept separate.

Although they are closely bonded to the application package objects, the configuration package objects should be kept as a separate class of objects. As a matter of good design, every software package should deny the ordinary user access to those objects that control the operating environment. This is done by creating a special set of configuration package objects that are only accessible by the **system administrator**. Since these objects are related to the design of the package, they may add one or more components to the source tree. In the last part of Chapter 8, we discuss this subject in more detail.

1.6   A Sample Product

Although the building of a software package could be defined in abstract terms and unrelated examples, it would be difficult to see and comprehend the total process. Instead, we will use a more concrete and realistic example of how the build process works. In *Source*

File Management with SCCS, the complete source for a source file management package was provided. Figure 1.4 shows the source tree for this software package. Although having the source files gives a clearer understanding about building a software package, they are not necessary. For the benefit of those readers who have the source files, any changes to the source files needed to implement the concepts presented in this book are described in the footnotes. Also, any new source files are described in the appendixes.

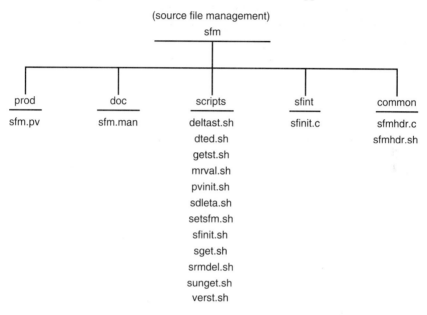

Figure 1.4 Source Tree for Example Software Package

1.7 Summary

This book is about transforming source files into a software package. The source files are transformed by various software tools. This transformation of source files into a finished product is called the **build process**. The **build instructions** define the build process by telling us how to use the software tools to build the software package. If the build process works correctly, then the same source files plus the same tools controlled by the same build instructions will always produce the same software package. Furthermore, when a source file changes, only those package objects that are affected will change. By doing this, we limit the number of package objects that must be verified.

We build package objects. A package object is a component of the software package. These components are built from source files, subcomponents, and other components, as described by the structure of the source tree. A subcomponent has the characteristics of a component, but only exists in order to build a single component. Also, we may build components, such as an object library, that is used to build other components. Such a component may or may not be a package object. Thus, if any source file, subcomponent, or component changes, all package objects affected by the change must also change. However, for the developer's convenience, the subcomponent may be the smallest buildable unit. Of course, the job is not finished until all package objects that are affected have been built.

The package objects can be classed as application package objects, maintenance package objects, or configuration package objects. How to write maintenance package objects and configuration package objects is given additional attention in this work.

CHAPTER 2

The UNIX Solution

2.1   Introduction

The building of a software package can be defined by the following formula:

```
source files + tools + build instructions = software package
```

In Chapter 1, we defined the *build process* as consisting of the **tools** plus the instructions on how to use those tools. While it is possible to build a software package as a single unit, we showed how this process can be partitioned into smaller divisions called components and subcomponents. A subset of these components represents package objects.

In this chapter, we take a brief look at how this knowledge above can be put into practice using the software tools provided with UNIX. We will then take a quick look at how the **make** command provides a formal language for defining the build instructions. Once we know how to build the application package objects, we then review how to build maintenance package objects and configuration package objects. Finally, we briefly discuss modifying an object file and building library files. The information provided in this chapter will be discussed in greater detail in the remainder of this work.

2.2   Objectives of the Build Process

In building a software package, we want to achieve certain objectives. In the same way that definitive objectives allow us to decide on the correctness of a program, we need definitive objectives to determine the correctness of the build process. To define the objectives, we need to have a concept of the software development environment. For our purposes, we assume the following:

1. The source files for a software package reside in a **source file library**. As stated in Chapter 1, there is a distinction between the SCCS source tree, kept in the source file library, and the work source tree, kept in a build directory. To preserve source file security and integrity, we will not build a software package in the SCCS source tree, nor will we keep SCCS files in the work source tree.

2. In our organization, the *development group* will develop, build, and verify the software package. When they feel that it is ready to be released, they will check all the source files into the source file library. The *configuration management group* will retrieve the file from the source file library and then build the package to verify that they can obtain the same results as the development group. The package built by the configuration management group will then be given to the *software assurance group* to verify that the package works according to the specifications. If the package passes the verification step, it will be made available to the *software users*. Figure 2.1 shows these relationships among the groups. Although the names of the groups may change from one organization to another, the functions performed exist in every organization.

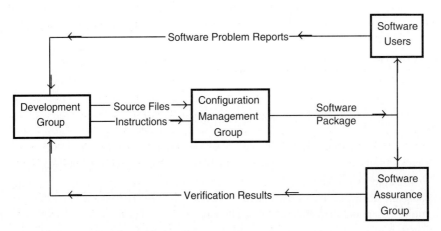

Figure 2. 1 Software Development Environment

Within this environment, we want the build process to fulfill the following objectives:

1. Building of the software package should require minimal written instructions. Ideally, building a software package would require two steps: (a) retrieval of the work source tree from the source file library; and (b) execution of the build instructions.

2. It should be possible to build either the entire software package, a component, or, if defined, a subcomponent.

3. Between each build, only the package objects that have changed need rebuilding. Changes that affect package objects are not limited to source files, but include changes to related components and subcomponents. For example, a component may be a module common to many package objects. If this component changes, then all package objects that use the component must change. By only building what has changed, we minimize the time it takes to build a software package.

4. The requirement specified in item 3 should also apply between releases of a software package. This should be true even if the package has to be retrieved from the source file library. While it reduces the time it takes to build a software package, this is not the primary purpose of this objective. The main purpose is to reduce the amount of time needed to verify the new version.

5. Since the work source tree may be attached to any directory, the build process must not be dependent on explicit path names.

6. Version management must apply to the tools used to build the software package. Although they are the active agents in the transformation of source files to package objects, the tools used to build a software package are rarely controlled. While the impact of a change in the tools used to build a package may be difficult to quantify, it cannot be ignored.

7. We must be aware that the build process plays a critical role in the building of zero-defect software. *Perfect source files built imperfectly result in an imperfect software package.*

2.3 "make": The Language for Building Software

Without doubt, the **make** utility is one of the most powerful software development tools in the UNIX toolkit. Being a special command processor, the **make** utility uses commands, called **make rules**, to describe the process for building software or documents. A make rule is composed of several lines that define the commands for the software tools and the interrelationship of the elements used to build an object. The make rules are contained in a file called the **makefile**.

How to write make rules and to use **make** is the subject of Chapters 3 through 6. After a brief introduction to **make**, Chapter 3 describes the basics for writing a **makefile**. In Chapter 4, we learn how the **make** command processes the **makefile** and how the default order of processing can be altered. From the simple **makefile**s of Chapter 3, the next step is to learn how to write more general and powerful **makefile**s; this is the topic of Chapter 5. In Chapter 6, the knowledge gained from Chapters 3 through 5 will be applied to the example software presented in Chapter 1. This will complete our discussion of how to write build instructions. Our discussion of the build process is completed in Chapter 7 when we discuss version control for software tools.

2.4 Software Package Administration

To this point, our main concern has been with the build process. The examples shown in Chapters 3 through 7 relate to *application package objects*. However, to be usable, application package objects must be installed on a system and configured to that machine's environment. Under the general rubric of software package administration, we discuss how to build maintenance package objects and configuration package objects in Chapter 8.

Software package maintenance has evolved from copying files to the **install** command of UNIX SVR3 to an entire set of packaging commands in UNIX SVR4. In this work, we are concerned with the principles of package maintenance. Therefore, instead of discussing the packaging command in UNIX SVR4, we will discuss how to interface with the *Software Management Option* of the **sysadm** command (added to UNIX System V in Release 2.0).

Even after a software package has been installed on a machine, there are tasks that occasionally must be done by the System Administrator. Since the average user need not know about these commands, they should be part of a menu that is only available to the System Administrator. Again, the **sysadm** command provides a solution through interface to the *Package Management Option*. This topic is also covered in Chapter 8.

We also face the additional problem of managing the differences in source files that may occur because of the software package being built for different machines or different customers. As an alternative to keeping multiple renditions of the source file and managing them through different branches in the SCCS file, we can take advantage of the macro processors provided by UNIX. In Chapter 9, we show how to control the build process with **cpp**, **vc**, or **m4**.

By the end of Chapter 9, we will be ready to build a software package that can be developed on one machine, built on another machine, and installed on a third machine. After all, in today's world, the environment shown in Figure 2.1 could be implemented on one machine or several machines. In addition, it is possible to require that the same source files build software packages for different types of machines and for different customers. By using the methods described in this book, the management of a complex environment becomes a feasible task.

2.5   Modifying an Object File

Once we know how to build a standard software package, we will then be ready to discuss special issues that affect the build process. In Chapter 10, we look at the tools that can be used to modify an object file and discuss both how and when to use the tools.

In Chapter 10 we will see that the compiler's link edit phase is not the end of the road for an object module. We can still reduce the size of an object module by (**strip**)ping the symbol table and debugging information. For some object modules, we can also reduce the size by removing duplicate structure and union descriptors with the **cprs** command.

Starting with UNIX System V Release 3.0, the *.comment* section has become a standard part of the Common Object File Format (COFF). Support of this new feature has added the *#ident* to the list of predefined macros for **cpp** and has added the **mcs** (Modify Comment Section) command to the list of UNIX utilities.

2.6   Using and Building Library Files

Every time we compile a program, we use an *archive library file*. Yet, little is said in the standard UNIX literature about how to control which library files are used in the build process. Even less attention is paid to how to build an archive library file. In Chapter 11, we try to rectify the problem by providing all the necessary information needed to build an archive library file.

Besides the standard archive library file, starting with UNIX System V Release 3.0, we can now use and build a *shared library file*. The *shared library* concept provides for the loading of library routines when the object module is executed. Not only does this reduce the disk space required by an object module, but it may also reduce memory requirements, since the text portion of a shared library is shared by different processes. How to use and build a shared library is also discussed in Chapter 11.

2.7   The Final Result

The examples given in the appendixes connect the preceding topics into one integrated build process that is a component of the software package in and of itself. Beginning with Appendix B, each appendix describes a single component of the software package for the source file management system shown in Figure 12.1. The difference between this figure and Figure 1.4 is the addition of the elements necessary to turn a software application into a software package. Furthermore, it makes no difference whether this software package is used by a single customer in your company or is distributed as a software product to many customers. The question is not the number of customers, but how we view the process of building software.

2.8   Summary

We have described the steps we will be taking in building the software package described in Chapter 1 according to the requirements defined. This objective will be completed in Chapter 7. We then take these application package objects and, by the end of Chapter 9, turn them into a software package that can be distributed on any number of machines.

In Chapter 10, we clean up the object files and take advantage of the new.*comment* section to track information about the module. In Chapter 11, we build an archive library. In addition, we show how to use and build a shared library using the same routines that we used to build the archive library. By the end of this work, we will have tackled almost every problem that occurs in the building of a software package. The results of this effort are shown in the examples presented in the appendixes.

CHAPTER 3

Writing "makefiles":
The Basics

3.1   Overview of the "make" Utility

Just as **shell** processes shell commands, **make** processes make commands called **make rules**. These rules take the form of **targets**, **dependencies**, and **command lines**. The **target**, the identifier for a specific make rule, defines what is to be made. One way to understand the idea of a **target** is to think of it as one option in a list of options (targets). As we shall see, these options can be either explicit or implicit. The **command lines** are the shell commands associated with the target (option).

   The notion of **dependencies** is a major reason **make** is more than a shell script with a case statement defining a list of options (targets). The **make** utility looks at the dependencies and checks to see if any of the dependencies have a modification time more recent than that of the target. If anything has a newer time, then **make** executes the commands associated with the target. This is the essential idea of **make**. Before looking at this idea in more detail, let's look what causes the **make** utility to be so valuable.

3.2   Importance of the "make" Utility

The **make** utility has become such an integral part of software development under UNIX that we often forget the various roles served by **make**. Although the following list is not inclusive, it reminds us of the central role played by **make** in the building of software packages:

   1. **make** *saves time:* Once we define the commands required to build a particular target, we can execute them by merely typing the following command line:

```
make {target}
```

Not only does it save the time required to type the command to build that particular target, but it also saves the time required to type the commands to check and build all the dependencies. In other words, enter the rules once, and use them repeatedly.

2. **make** *reduces the chance of making an error:* Occasionally, we make errors when typing a command line, but these are not the only errors that can be made. In a software project involving many package objects, one can easily forget all the dependencies to each package object. Since we assume that we correctly built the package object, we first question our change. Only after wasting much time looking at the source code, do we question whether the individual components represent the latest version. Once the commands associated with a particular target are correct and the dependencies correctly defined, **make** ensures that nothing is forgotten.

3. *Reproducibility:* If written correctly, the **makefile** comprises the complete instructions on how to build a software package from a given set of source files with a given set of tools. In Chapter 2, we defined the formula for building a software package as follows:

```
source files + tools + build instructions =software package
```

Since we will use **makefiles** to describe the build instructions, we can rewrite the formula as follows:

```
source files + tools + makefiles = software package
```

Thus, if we had control over the version of the source files, tools (see Chapter 7), and **makefiles** used in building the software package, we could build an identical version at any time.

Now that we understand the basic idea of **make** and the purpose of **make**, it is time to discuss the details. We start with the definition of the **make rule** and then proceed to expand on this definition.

3.3   The "make rule"

The **make rule** is the heart of the **make** utility. This rule has the following format:

```
{target ...} :[:] [{dependency ...}] [# comment]
[<tab>[-][@]{command line1} [# comment]]
[<tab>[-][@]{command line2} [# comment]]
    .
    .
    .
```

Or the entire rule can be stated on a single line with the following format:

```
{target ...} :[:] [{dependency ...}] [; cmnd line] [# comment]
```

Every **makefile**, the source file for **make**, contains one or more **make rule**s. Since the **{target ...}** identifies the rule, it must be present. However, the **{dependency ...}** and the **{command line}** are optional. Thus, a make rule may consist of a target and a dependency, a target and command lines, or all three elements. Because of their close relationship (see Section 3.3.1), the target plus the dependency is called the **dependency line**.

Naming Conventions: The names for targets and dependencies follow the rules for the naming of files. However, the '**=**', '**:**', and '**@**' have special meanings and *must not* be used in macro names (see Section 3.3.1) or names on the dependency line.

Continuation of a Line: It is possible to continue a noncomment line by using a backslash followed by a newline. When **make** processes the line, a single space will replace the backslash, newline, and the leading blanks and tabs of the next line.

3.3.1 Dependency Line

The results of the evaluation of the dependency line determine whether the target is out of date. In actuality, this test is the core of **make**. As shown in the preceding syntax statement, one or two colons separate the targets from the dependencies. For the simple makefiles described in this chapter, we only need the single- colon syntax. In Chapter 5, the purpose of single- versus double-colon syntax will be discussed. So, for the simple **make rule**, the format of the dependency line is as follows:

```
{target ...} : [{dependency ...}]
```

The makefile shown in Figure 3.1 will be used as the starting point for discussion. It is a simple makefile with only six make rules. Everything is explicitly defined so that we can clearly see the relationships. As we learn more about **make**, the **makefile** will continue to become more compact and more flexible.

For readers who want a more visual demonstration of how **make** works, Figures 3.2 through 3.5 show sample source files for pgm1.c, pgm2.c, moda.c, and modb.c. When you enter the text shown in Figure 3.1, the file name must be either **makefile** or **Makefile**. Since, in this chapter, our discussion is limited to explicit make rules, the following **make** command syntax must be used to process the example makefiles:

```
make -r [{target}] [{macro definitions}]
```

The **-r** option suppresses the use of **make**'s built-in rules, also called implicit make rules (see Section 5.4.8 for more details). Since the implicit make rules are being suppressed, **make** will issue the following message: **No suffix list.** Ignore the message; everything is fine

```
# An Example of a Simple Makefile
all : pgm1 pgm2 # Example of dependencies that are targets

pgm1 : pgm1.c moda.o
        cc -o pgm1 moda.o pgm1.c # comments can appear here

pgm2 : pgm2.c moda.o modb.o
        cc -o pgm2 moda.o modb.o pgm2.c

moda.o : moda.c
        cc -c moda.c

modb.o : modb.c
        cc -c modb.c

clean :
        -rm -f moda.o modb.o # Leading - means ignore errors
        -rm -f pgm1.o pgm2.o pgm1 pgm2
        @echo "work files removed" # The @ means don't print
```

Figure 3.1 A Simple Makefile

```
/* pgm1.c - Example program for learning about make */
#include <stdio.h>

main()
{
        printf("Test Program 1\n");
        testa();
}
```

Figure 3.2 Source for pgm1.c

```
/* pgm2.c - Example program for learning about make */
#include <stdio.h>

main()
{
       printf("Test Program 2\n");
       testa();
       testb();
}
```

Figure 3.3 Source for pgm2.c

```
/* moda.c - Example for learning how make works */
#include <stdio.h>

testa()
{
       printf("Module A test\n");
}
```

Figure 3.4 Source for moda.c

```
/* modb.c - Example for learning how make works */
#include <stdio.h>

testb()
{
       printf("Module B test\n");
}
```

Figure 3.5 Source for moda.b

What Is a Target?

The **target** identifies a make rule. As shown in Figure 3.1, a makefile may include many make rules. By default, **make** processes only the first explicit make rule. However, we can override the default by specifying the target, or targets, to be made on the **make** command line. Thus, all the following are valid expressions of what can be made from the makefile shown in Figure 3.1:

```
make                      (will make the target "all" by default)
make pgm1                 (will make the target "pgm1")
make moda.o               (will make the target "moda.o")
make modb.o               (will make the target "modb.o")
make moda.o modb.o        (will make both "moda.o" and "modb.o")
make clean                (will make the target "clean")
```

> **Note:** If **make** cannot find the target name specified, it will fail with the following error message:
>
> **Make. Don't know how to make <target name>**

Although Figure 3.1 only shows single target names for each make rule, more than one target name can identify the same make rule. For example, the following is a valid dependency line:

```
pgm1 pgm2 : moda.o modb.o
```

The use of multiple target names for a single make rule will become more important as we start modifying the rules to make them more general. For the time being, all we need to know is that the {**target ...**} can be a single target name or a list of target names.

What Is a Dependency?

Simply stated, the target depends on the files or other make rules listed as dependencies. The dependency name, which can be either a file name or a target name, identifies dependencies. For example, in Figure 3.1, the target called pgm1 is dependent on pgm1.c and moda.o. We can see that one dependency name is a file name (pgm1.c) and one is a target name (moda.o).

> **Note:** The include file, stdio.h, is not considered a dependency. To qualify as a dependency, a source file or object file should be within the domain of the software package. Files outside this domain should be considered as part of the tools to build a software package and controlled accordingly (See Chapter 7).

3.3.2 Target–Dependency Relationship

The objective of the target - dependency relationship is to determine whether the target is out of date. This is accomplished by comparing each dependency name with the target name. If the dependency name is a target name, the associated make rule must be evaluated. This hierarchical evaluation of dependency names can be shown as a **dependency tree.** The resolution of all the dependencies for the target "all" in Figure 3.1 requires the evaluation of the dependency tree shown in Figure 3.6.

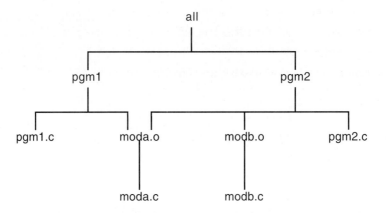

Figure 3.6 Resolution of Dependency for the Target "all"

Using Figure 3.6 as an example, the following describes the tests made by the **make** command to check the dependency line:

1. For every dependency name listed, **make** checks to see if the dependency name matches the target name of another make rule. When the dependency name matches a target name, the dependency line for this target must be checked for target names. This process repeats itself until the dependencies for the new target name either have no associated targets or the new target name has no dependencies. Once all the dependency names have been evaluated, **make** proceeds with comparing the target name to the dependency names.

   For example, starting with the target "all," the dependencies pgm1 and pgm2 have associated target names. Following the trail for pgm1 (pgm2 would be similar), the dependencies for pgm1 include a target for moda.o. Since the dependency for moda.o does not have an associated target, we can proceed with the next level of testing.

2. Once all the dependencies have been checked, **make** tries to find a file name that matches the target name. If one is not found, the target is considered out of date and the command lines are executed. For example, if the file moda.o does not exist in the current working directory, the target is marked as out of date and the command lines are executed.

3. Conversely, if a file with the same name as that of the target exists and there are no dependencies, the target is considered current. For example, in Figure 3.1, if a file called "clean" somehow came into being, the commands associated with this target would never be executed since the target would always be current.

4. If a file with the same name as the target does exist, the modification time of the target file name is compared to the modification time of each dependency name. For example, the modification time for the file moda.o would be compared with the modification time for the dependent file moda.c. If the modification time of

any dependency is more recent than the modification time of the target, the target is considered out of date and the command lines are executed.

5. If the target tested was a dependency of another dependency line under evaluation, processing of the original dependency line continues at step 1. This cycle repeats until all dependencies in the dependency tree have been resolved and the original target has been tested.

6. If **make** cannot resolve the dependency name to a file name or a target name, it will display the following error message:

```
Make.  Don't know how to make <target name>.
```

For example, if the file moda.c did not exist, **make** would fail with the message.

```
Make.  Don't know how to make moda.c.
```

Dependencies are resolved according to the order in which they are listed. In this sense, the dependency line is like a conditional statement and can be stated in the following formula:

```
if Date_of_Target < (Date_of_Dependency-1 or
                      Date_of_Dependency-2 or
                      ...
                      Date_of_Dependency-n)
do commands
```

3.3.3 Dummy Target

A **dummy target** is a target that will never actually be built. In Figure 3.1, the "all" and "clean" are examples of dummy targets. For the target "all," there are no associated commands to build the target. Its sole purpose is to force the testing of both pgm1 and pgm2. However, "clean" always executes the associated command lines, but it does not build the target.

When a dummy target is a dependency to another target, it will always be considered newer than the associated target. This means that the command lines associated with a dependency line that include a dummy target as a dependency name will always be executed. Thus, in the following example, the command lines for pgm1 would always be executed even though no changes were made to any of the source files:

```
pgm1 : pgm1.c dummy
        (command line 1)
        (command line 2)
dummy :
        (command line 3)
```

3.3.4 Command Lines

One or more command lines may be associated with each dependency line. The command lines are executed when the dependency line tests consider the target to be out of date. The command line itself is equivalent to a one-line shell script. Thus, multiple command lines equate to an equal number of independent shell scripts. A make rule expressed in shell commands would be roughly equivalent to the following:

```
if test $TARDATE < $DEPDATE
then
(Command Line 1)
(Command Line 2)
       .
       .
       .

fi
```

For example, if the task had to be executed in another directory, the following make rule would be correct:

```
pgm1 : ../test/junk.c pgm1.c
        cd ../test; cc -c junk.c
```

> **Note:** One should always think of every command line as a one-line shell script. With only a few variations (see the following discussion of macros), whatever can be done on a one-line shell script can be done on the command line. Also, like shell scripts, the environment of one command line is not passed to the next command line.

Just as in shell programming, a single logical line can be broken into multiple physical lines by escaping the newline. Thus, the preceding example could be rewritten as

```
pgm1 : ../test/junk.c pgm1.c
        cd ../test; \
           cc -c junk.c
```

When a command line returns a nonzero return code, **make** skips the remaining lines in the make rule and abandons the processing of any other make rules. By prefixing a command line with a '-', a nonzero return code would be ignored by **make**. For example, the "clean" target shown in Figure 3.1 has the **rm** command lines prefixed with a '-'. If the error return codes were not ignored and moda.o and modb.o were not found, the files for pgm1 and pgm2 would never be removed.

The **-i** and **-k** options of the **make** command (see Chapter 4) and the **.IGNORE** target (see Special Targets in Chapter 5) also modify the default method of handling errors. However, these options affect the entire makefile, whereas, the '**-**' affects only the prefixed line.

By default, **make** prints every command line before it is executed. In the most cases, this is perfectly acceptable. However, at times this causes a problem. For example, when using the **echo** command, the argument for the **echo** command prints twice. By prefixing the line with an '**@**' (see the **echo** command line in Figure 3.1), the printing of the command will be suppressed and only the message will be printed.

The printing of command lines by **make** can also be suppressed by the **-s** option of the **make** utility (see Chapter 4) and the **.SILENT** target (see Special Targets in Chapter 5). These options apply to the entire makefile and will suppress the printing of all command lines.

Both the '**-**' and '**@**' may be present on the same command line. They must appear immediately after the tab character. However, the order of appearance is not important

---

3.3.5 A Short Demonstration

Using the information supplied so far, let's see how it is applied in different situations. As you execute the following steps, compare the results with the rules stated for dependency lines and command lines. Understanding the preceding discussion is important, because the rest of **make** is nothing more than variations on these themes. As stated previously, **make** requires the **-r** option to suppress the execution of implicit make rules that may affect the results of the following demonstration.

Step 1: To make sure that we start from a known environment, remove all files except the source files with the following command:

```
make -r clean
```

Step 2: Now we will build both pgm1 and pgm2 by executing the following command:

```
make -r all
```

Watch the sequence of events and compare them with the chart in Figure 3.6. First moda.c is compiled to create moda.o. Next, pgm1 is made. Since moda.o already exists and is newer than moda.c, this step is skipped in making pgm2. Only modb.c needs to be compiled before compiling pgm2.

Step 3: To see what happens when a target is current, execute the following command:

```
make -r pgm1
```

The make utility displays the message:

```
'pgm1' up to date.
```

Step 4: However, if the target is a dummy target, then no message is displayed. To prove this, execute the command:

```
make -r all
```

Why is this so? Since there is no matching file name, a dummy target is never up to date, although the dependencies may be up to date.

Step 5: To see what happens when a source file changes, execute the following sequence of commands:

```
touch -m moda.c
make -r all
```

The **touch** command alters the modification date of the file moda.c to the current date and time. This forces moda.o to be out of date and, in turn, pgm1 and pgm2. Notice that modb.o does not have to be made, since it is current.

Step 6: For a demonstration of **make**'s selectivity in updating, a different source file will be modified. Execute the following commands and note what happens:

```
touch -m modb.c
make -r all
```

Now that modb.c is newer than modb.o, modb.o is recompiled and, as a result, pgm2 is also recompiled. As expected, pgm1 does not change since it is not dependent on modb.o.

Step 7: A file is never created for a dummy target. To see what happens when a file has the same name as a dummy target, execute the following commands:

```
touch -c clean
make -r clean
rm -f clean
```

Since there are no dependencies, the target will always be considered up to date. Thus, the commands for this target will never be executed.

Now that we have an understanding of the key principle of **make**, we can proceed to add additional features. As we proceed, our simple example will become more flexible.

3.4   Comments in "makefiles"

With one exception, a comment can appear anywhere within a makefile. A comment begins with a pound sign (#) and ends with a newline. The one exception is that a command line comment cannot start immediately after the initial tab character. After the tab, **make** expects a command and not a comment. Figure 3.1 shows several examples of how comments can be used.

Note: Except for the command line, **make** always considers the pound sign (#) to be the beginning of a comment. In addition, no facility has been provided to escape the pound sign. Thus, the pound sign (#) cannot be used in a macro definition line (see Section 3.5.1).

3.5   Using Macros in "makefiles"

Using the **macro** facility of **make** allows us to write more flexible and more readable makefiles. How a **macro** works is very simple. The **macro definition** replaces every occurrence of a **macro name** in a dependency line or a command line. This allows for the parameterization of the makefile, which in turn reduces the effort required to incorporate changes. The following sections show how to define and use macros in makefiles.

3.5.1 Macro Definition

The following defines the syntax for a **macro**:

```
{macro name} = {macro definition}
```

Just as a ':' defines a line as a dependency line and an initial tab defines a command line, the equal sign (=) declares to **make** that this line is a **macro definition line**. The {macro name} is a string of any alphabetic or numeric characters and must not contain a metacharacter ($, @, #, =, *, &, ( ), { }, <tab>, or <space>) recognized by **make**.

The {macro definition} can be any string of characters, except a pound sign (#). Since **make** ignores any tabs or spaces surrounding the equal sign, the first character after the equal sign that is not a tab or a space marks the beginning of the macro definition. A newline terminates the macro definition. If, after removing any tabs or spaces, there are no characters following the equal sign, the definition is called a *null definition*.

The following are examples of valid macros:

```
PGM1 = pgm1
PGM2 = pgm2
OBJECTS = moda.o modb.o
```

3.5.2 Use of Macros

To use a **macro name**, the name must be prefixed by a '**$**' and, if the name is not a single character, it must be enclosed in either parentheses (( )) or braces ({ }). The following are a few examples of how to use macro names:

```
PGMS = $(PGM1) ${PGM2}


$(PGM2) : $(OBJECTS) $(PGM2).
        ${CC} ${CFLAGS} -o ${PGM2} ${OBJECTS} ${PGM2}.c

clean :
        -rm ${OBJECTS}
        -rm ${PGMS}
```

> **Note:** If the '$' needs to be protected, it can be escaped by having two dollar signs in a row: '$$'. When the token is evaluated, the first '$' will be discarded.
>
> Although either parentheses (( )) or braces ({ }) may be used to delineate macro names, parentheses are also used to delineate shell variables and member names of archive libraries. To avoid confusion, we recommend that braces be used to delineate macro names, as is the practice in this work.

Although they look very similar, it is important to understand the difference between a **macro** and a **variable**. A **macro** means to replace the **macro name** with the **macro definition**. In a sense, it is like editing the text and substituting one string for another. After the substitution has taken place, the original **macro name** no longer appears in the text. For example, the line:

```
PGMS = ${PGM1} ${PGM2}
```

would become:

```
PGMS = pgm1 pgm2
```

A variable means to use the value defined by the **variable name**. Thus, the **variable name** does not disappear when the text is processed. Since the **variable name** remains as part of the text, it can be changed during the processing of the file (for example, shell variables).

When executed, the makefile shown in Figure 3.7 illustrates how **make** processes macros. Assuming it is executed in a directory with 'C' source files, the command:

make -r

causes the following to be printed by **make**:

```
No suffix list.
      echo EST1
EST1
      echo *.c
moda.c modb.c pgm1.c pgm2.c
      echo string 2
string 2
      echo Any valid character string plus more
Any valid  character string plus more
```

```
TEST1 = Any valid character string
TEST2 = *.c
TEST3 = string 1
TEST4 = ${TEST1} plus more

TEST1  : ${TEST2}
        echo $TEST1
        echo ${TEST2}
        echo ${TEST3}
        echo ${TEST4}

TEST3 = string 2
```

Figure 3.7 A Makefile to Demonstrate the Use of Macros

Comparing the results with the make rules in the **makefile**, the following observations about the behavior of **macro**s can be made:

1. The position in the makefile in which a macro is defined is not important. If position were important, then the command line "echo ${TEST3}" would have been expanded to "echo string 1".

2. When multiple definitions exist for the same macro name, only the last definition will be used.

3. Macros can be used in the definition of other macros (see the macro definition line for TEST4).

4. The macro name alone (without the required delimiters) does not cause the replacement of text. The target name TEST1 is an example of this principle.

5. A macro name that has no corresponding macro definition line is treated as having a null definition. In the command line "echo $TEST1", the macro name

would be $T, since TEST1 was not enclosed by '( )' or '{ }'. Since a macro defini-
tion line for $T does not exist, the line evaluates as "echo EST1".

Note: The use of capital letters in macro names is not required. This practice merely helps to identify the name as a macro name.

Using the macro features described, the makefile shown in Figure 3.1 could be modified to look like the one shown in Figure 3.8. Although a bit complicated, this makefile
illustrates several very important features of macros. In the macro definition lines for
OBJS and PGMS, we see how macros can be used in the definition of other macros. We
also see that macros can be used for target names and dependency names, as well as on the
command line. With this basic knowledge of macros, we can precede to more variations
on how to use them.

3.5.3 Internal Macros

Except for dummy targets, the objective of the command lines associated with a target is
to build the named target. Thus, the command line normally contains reference to the target name. In Figure 3.8, this reference was established by defining macros for each target
name. Although this method works, it becomes very cumbersome in a large makefile. To
solve this problem, **make** provides the **$@** internal macro.

The **$@** macro refers to the current target name. For a make rule with a single target
name, it always refers to that target name. However, for make rules with multiple target
names, the **$@** refers to the target being built. For example, in the following make rule,
$@ could refer to either **target1** or **target2**.

```
target1 target2 :
        cc -o $@ $@.c
```

The command:

```
make target1
```

results in the following command line expansion:

```
cc -o target1 target1.c
```

Yet the command:

```
make target1 target2
```

```
# An Example of a Simple Makefile with Macros
MODA = moda
MODB = modb
OBJS = ${MODA}.o ${MODB}.o
PGM1 = pgm1
PGM2 = pgm2
PGMS = ${PGM1} ${PGM2}

all : ${PGMS}

${PGM1} : ${PGM1}.c ${MODA}.o
        cc -o ${PGM1} ${MODA}.o ${PGM1}.c

${PGM2} : ${PGM2}.c ${OBJS}
        cc -o ${PGM2} ${OBJS} ${PGM2}.c

${MODA}.o : ${MODA}.c
        cc -c ${MODA}.c

${MODB}.o : ${MODB}.c
        cc -c ${MODB}.c

clean :
        -rm -f ${OBJS} ${PGMS} ${PGM1}.o ${PGM2}.o
        @echo "work files removed"
```

Figure 3.8   Figure 3.1 with Macros

results in the following commands being executed:

```
cc -o target1 target1.c
cc -o target2 target2.c
```

If **make** does not support variables, how can the latter be accomplished? Without getting into all the details that will be discussed in Chapter 4, **make** roughly uses the following sequence of events:

1. All macro definitions are resolved.

2. Any macros in dependency lines are expanded.

3. The targets to be made are resolved.

4. The internal macros are defined.

5. The internal macros in dependency lines are expanded.

6. The dependency lines are checked for out-of-date targets.

7. For out-of-date targets, the macros in the command lines are expanded before execution.

8. The expanded command lines are executed.

We see from this sequence of events that the internal macros are dynamically defined during the execution of the makefile. Thus, the preceding example for multiple target names is correctly resolved because the $@ macro (step 4) is before the expansion of the command line (step 7).

The $@ macro also can be used to define dependencies. However, since the $@ macro is not defined until step 4, it must be escaped to avoid premature expansion in step 2. As discussed previously, we solve this by adding another '$' to the internal macro. For example, the dependency on the corresponding C source file could be written as follows:

```
target1 target2 : $$@.c
        cc -o $@ $@.c
```

Without the $@ macro, the preceding would require two make rules to correctly describe the relationship between the target and the dependency. Although the makefile in Figure 3.8 does not have multiple targets with common dependencies, we can take still take advantage of the $@ macro. Modifying the makefile in Figure 3.8 to use the $@ macro, we obtain the makefile in Figure 3.9.

Figure 3.9 illustrates an important limitation of the $@ macro. Whereas the $@ macro works fine for targets without suffixes (pgm1 and pgm2), we must be careful with targets that have suffixes (moda.o and modb.o). We will discuss how to strip the suffix in Chapter 5 when we discuss macro string substitution.

The $? internal macro can also be used in writing command lines for explicit make rules. The $? macro defines a list of dependency names that are newer than the target. In the following example, the names of the object modules that caused the command lines to be executed would be displayed:

```
pgm1: $$@.c moda.o modb.o
        @echo Revised modules are $?
        cc -o $@ moda.o modb.o $@.c
```

The $? macro is also very useful in maintaining archive library files, as the following example shows:

```
libfoo.a : $ {OBJECTS}
        ar  rc  $@  $?
```

```
# An Example of a Simple Makefile with internal macros
MODA = moda
MODB = modb
OBJS = ${MODA}.o ${MODB}.o
PGMS = pgm1 pgm2
POBJS = pgm1.o pgm2.o

all : ${PGMS}

pgm1 : $$@.c ${MODA}.o
        cc -o $@ ${MODA}.o $@.c

pgm2 : $$@.c ${OBJS}
        cc -o $@ ${OBJS} $@.c

${MODA}.o : ${MODA}.c
        cc -c ${MODA}.c

${MODB}.o : ${MODB}.c
        cc -c ${MODB}.c

clean :
        -rm -f ${OBJS} ${POBJS} ${PGMS}
        @echo "work files removed"
```

Figure 3.9 Figure 3.1 with Internal Macros

3.5.4 Environmental Variables as Macros

Besides the internal macros and the macros defined in the makefile, **make** automatically defines the current **environmental variables** as macros. As the following example shows, we can use this facility to pass information to **make**:

```
${PGM} : $$@.c
        cc -o $@ $@.c
```

Without a definition for ${PGM}, this makefile would fail. However, the following command will execute correctly:

```
$ PGM=pgm1; export PGM; make
```

On most versions of UNIX, the following shorter form of this command also works:

```
$ PGM=pgm1 make
```

This shorter version passes **PGM** to **make** as an environmental variable without having to export it to the environment. For conciseness, the shorter notation will be used in this work.

Should a macro definition line match the environmental variable, the internal definition takes precedence. As we will see in Chapter 4, this order can be changed so that the definition provided by the environmental variable has precedence.

3.6   "make" Interface to the Shell

In Section 3.3.4, we said that command lines are, in actuality, one-line shell scripts. Now that we have been through all the basic components of a makefile, it is time to take a more detailed look at the interface to the shell. In particular, the shell file name metacharacters, shell variables, and the execution of shell commands interest us.

3.6.1 Shell File Name Metacharacters

Shell uses the characters '*', '?', and '[ ]' for pattern matching against file names.[1] As a single shell script, the command line's use of metacharacters is the same as any shell script. For example, when processing the makefile in Figure 3.7, the command '**echo *.c**' passes to the shell without the expansion of the file names.

The unique feature is that metacharacters can also be used to define dependencies on the dependency line. For example, the following is a valid dependency line that uses metacharacters:

```
pgm2  :  $$@.c mod[ab].c
        lpr $?
```

As shown for the ${TEST2} macro in Figure 3.7, the use of shell metacharacters as part of a macro definition is also permissible.

> **Note:** Dependency names that include shell metacharacters are expanded simultaneously with the internal macros.

3.6.2 Using Shell Variables

Although shell variables cannot be used in dependency lines, they can be used on command lines. However, since each command line represents a separate shell script, the variable cannot be set on one line and used on another line. This would be the equivalent of defining the variable in one shell script and using it in another shell script.

---

[1]The definitions for these shell metacharacters are beyond the scope of this book. If you are not sure of their definition or use, refer to the appropriate UNIX documentation or any introductory book on shell programming.

In Figure 3.7, we saw that the $T in the shell variable $TEST1 was considered a single-character macro. Just as we needed to escape the internal macro, the '$' of the shell variable must be escaped by another '$'. The following example shows how to define and use a shell variable:

```
test :
        foo='this is a test'; echo $$foo
```

Table 3.1 shows the variables set by shell that can be used in a command line. From this table, we can make several observations:

1. Everything from the leading tab to the newline is passed to the shell, including the '#'. Thus, the '#' on the command line is processed according to shell rules.

2. On the command line, there is a difference between **$@** (a **make** internal macro) and **$$@** (a shell variable). This is also true of the difference between **${TEST}** (a macro) and **$$TEST** (a shell variable). The differences can be shown by running the following makefile:

```
TEST=this is a test
junk : $$@.c TEST
        set $@.c; echo $$@

TEST :
        TEST="what a test"; export TEST; echo $$TEST
        echo ${TEST}
```

Although confusing to the reader, the name **TEST** can be used as a **macro name**, a **target name**, and a **shell variable name** without confusing **make**. Also, the variable **$$@** acts as an escaped **internal macro** when used on a dependency line and an escaped **shell variable** when used on a command line. Without question, the preceding makefile is confusing to read. However, when we forget to correctly separate macro names from shell variable names, we can confuse **make**.

3. Both dollar signs ($) must be escaped for the **$$** shell variable.

3.6.3 Execution of Command Lines

As with any shell, the command line must inherit an environment. In this case, the environment consists of the environmental variables inherited by **make** plus the variable **MAKEFLAGS** (see Chapter 5 for more information). To see the environmental variables inherited by the command line, create and make the following makefile:

```
environ :
        env
```

The **make** command does not provide a way to define a new environmental variable within a makefile. However, an environmental variable that existed when **make** was executed can be changed by a macro definition line. For example, the PATH variable may be defined to ensure a constant search path. To see what happens, modify the preceding makefile to look like the following:

```
PATH = /usr/bin:/bin:/etc
environ :
      env
```

With a little trickery, a macro definition can become the definition for an environmental variable. Try the following makefile and see what happens:

```
VARM = This is a test.
environ :
      VARE='${VARM}'; export VARE; env
```

Table 3.1 Valid Shell Internal Variables

Shell Variable	Example Command Line
$*	set *.c; echo $$*
$#	set *.c; echo $$#
$@	set *.c; echo $$@
$$	echo Process ID $$$$
$?	-false; echo $$?
$!	find $$HOME -name '*.c' > foo & $$!

3.7 Summary

There are three types of lines in a **makefile**: *dependency lines*, *command lines*, and *macro definition lines*. One or more command lines may be associated with a dependency line and will be executed only if the target is out of date with respect to the dependencies.

The dependency line and, optionally, one or more command lines define the **make rules**. Unless changed on the **make** command line, the default make rule to be made is the first make rule defined. After taking care of appropriate macro substitutions, the dependency names on the dependency lines are evaluated with respect to the modification time of the target being built. If the target is out of date, the command lines associated with the dependency line are executed. The command lines are individually passed to the shell. As a result, each command line needs to be viewed as a separate shell script. Although not required, the normal objective of the command line is to build the associated target. If it does not, then the target is called a **dummy target**.

To simplify makefiles to make them more flexible, **make** supports the use of **macros** (not to be confused with variables). Macros may be defined either on macro definition lines or as environmental variables and can be used on any line. Special **internal macros** (**$@** and **$?**) can also be used in the writing of makefiles.

The **shell file name metacharacters** ('*', '?', and '[ ]') can be used on both dependency lines and command lines. By escaping the '$' with another '$', it is possible to define **shell variables** and use the **shell internal variables** on the command lines.

Take the time to understand this chapter. It is the key to understanding how to use **make**. Chapters 4 and 5 will just expand on these basics to create more flexible and more powerful makefiles.

CHAPTER 4

Executing "makefiles": The "make" Command

4.1   Overview of the "make" Command

The **make** command interprets and executes the **make rules** in the **makefile**. Chapter 3 described how to write a simple makefile. How to take full advantage of the features of **make** will be described in Chapter 5. In this chapter, we discuss the **make** command itself. After a brief section covering the syntax of the **make** command, we discuss the default operation of **make**. In the remaining sections, we show how each option and argument modifies the default processing.

4.2   Syntax of the "make" Command

The format for the **make** command is as follows:

```
[environmental variable ...] make [-f {makefile}] [-e]
    [-r] [-i] [-k] [-t] [-n] [-b] [-p] [-s] [-q]
    [{macro definition} ...] [{target} ...]
```

4.3   The Default Operation of "make"

According to Bradford,[1] the execution of make proceeds in the following order:[2]

    1. The **MAKEFLAGS** environmental variable determines the initial execution environment. Normally, the MAKEFLAGS variable is only used in recursive

---

[1]E. G. Bradford, *An Augmented Version of MAKE* (Whippany, N.J.: Bell Laboratories, n.d.), p. 2.

[2]There are a few differences between what is stated by Bradford and the actual operation of the System V version of **make**. When this occurs (for example, the initial assignment for MAKEFLAGS), the text describes the System V action.

invocations of **make** (see Chapter 5 for more information). Thus, when executed from the shell command line, the **MAKEFLAGS** variable will not be defined. In this case, **make** defines the **MAKEFLAGS** variable with the **backward compatibility (b) flag** as the initial value: **(MAKEFLAGS=b)**.

2. The **make** command processes each character in the **MAKEFLAGS** variable as a keyletter option.

3. The command line is then read and any options present on the command line are processed. Except for the **-f**, **-r**, and **-p** options, which only apply to the current makefile, the minus sign is stripped and the option keyletter is concatenated to the **MAKEFLAGS** variable. For example, the command

```
$ make -k
```

results in the following definition for **MAKEFLAGS**:

```
MAKEFLAGS=bk
```

4. Any macro definitions specified on the command line are then processed. As we shall see in the following, these **command line macro definitions** are different from environmental variables and macro definitions defined within a makefile.

5. The default **macro definitions,** default **make rules**, default **inference rule**s, and default **suffix rules** are then processed. These defaults form what we will call the **internal description file**, to which the **makefile** is appended. The makeup of the internal description file is discussed in Chapter 5.

6. The **environmental variables** are then read and processed as macro definitions. The value defined by the environmental variable takes precedence over default macro definitions, but not over command line macro definitions. As we shall see, the environmental variables and the command line macro definitions jointly define the environmental variables inherited by the command lines.

All the preceding processing occurs before reading the makefile. The next phase is to read and process the makefile in the following order of events:

1. The **make** command searches the current working directory for a file named *makefile* or *Makefile*. If **make** cannot find either of these files, it searches for the files *s.makefile* or *s.Makefile*. Should one of these SCCS files be found, **make** will issue a **get** command to retrieve the default version of the makefile.[3] If **make** cannot find a makefile, it will fail with the following error message:

```
Make: No arguments or description file. Stop
```

---

[3]For more information about the default SID, see the manual page for the **get** command. In summary, unless the default SID flag has been set, the **get** command will retrieve the makefile that matches the condition of being the maximum release and the maximum level within that release.

> **Note:** Some implementations of **make**, upon the completion of the **make** command, remove a makefile that has been retrieved from an SCCS file.

2. On the first pass through a makefile, **make** processes the macro definition lines. When the macro names match, the macro definition line always replaces the default macro definition. By default, a macro definition line also replaces the definition for an environmental variable. However, the **-e** option (see Section 4.6.1) alters this precedence.

3. The **make** command then goes through the makefile one more time.In this pass, the macro definitions replace the macro names listed on the dependency lines. However, macro substitution for the command lines does not occur until they are executed.

After completing the housekeeping work, **make** starts processing the make rules. When no target names appear on the make command line, the first target in the makefile is processed. Although the processing of the dependencies for this target may reference other targets, **make** only processes this target. For example, the first make rule in Figure 3.9 is for the target name "all". Since this is a dummy target, the targets for "pgm1" and "pgm2" are always executed. However, if the first make rule has no dependencies, then only that make rule is executed. For example, if the first make rule in Figure 3.9 was:

```
help :
        @echo "The Great Pumpkin helps those \
              who help themselves."
```

then only the **echo** command would be executed.

Now that we understand the default actions of the **make** command, we can discuss how that action can be modified. The default action can be changed via flags, command line macro definitions, and the specification of target names. Since we often wish to begin with something other than the first target, Section 4.4 shows how this can be done.

4.4   Defining the Targets to be Processed

Target names can be viewed as keys to a menu of items that can be processed by **make**. We can choose a menu item by specifying the target name on the make command line. The format for this argument is as follows:

```
make [{target} ...]
```

The argument **{target}** can be any explicitly defined target or a target that can be made by using inference rules (see Chapter 5 for details). As the syntax shows, one or more **{target}** arguments can be specified on the command line. To get a better understanding of this option, let's look at a few examples.

As shown in Figure 3.9, no other target references the "clean" target. Thus, it can only be made by explicitly stating the target name, as in the following example:

```
$ make clean
```

Again using Figure 3.9, the command line

```
$ make pgm1 pgm2
```

is the equivalent to the default target for this makefile.

4.5   Changing the Input to "make"

In most situations, the default naming convention for makefiles works fine. However, when we need more than one makefile in a directory, they all cannot be called makefile. By using the **-f** option, we can tell **make** to use a different file name. The **-f** option also allows us to concatenate several makefiles into a single makefile. In addition, the minus sign, "-", redirects the input to the standard input. The following sections discuss these variations on the **-f** option in detail.

4.5.1 Handling "makefiles" with Different Names

On occasion, it may be necessary to use a different name for the makefile. The default search for file names may be overridden by using the **-f** option. The format of this option is:

```
-f {makefile}
```

where {**makefile**} is the file name of the makefile. For example, the following would use the file **gl.mk** as the makefile instead of **[mM]akefile**:

```
$ make -f gl.mk
```

Changing the makefile name affects the current invocation of make. Therefore, the flag and file name are not added to the **MAKEFLAGS** variable.

> **Note**: To identify a file as a makefile, a standard naming convention is important. One popular method adds a suffix to the name **"(Mm)akefile"** to create such names as **makefile.sun** or **makefile.vax**. Alternatively, the suffix ".mk" could be added to a descriptive name. For example, the names **gl.mk** and **moda.mk** would identify these files as makefiles.

4.5.2 Concatenating Several "makefiles"

There is a little-known feature of **make** that allows concatenation of several makefiles into a single makefile by using the **-f** flag. To illustrate this feature, let us split the makefile shown in Figure 3.9 into two parts. We will call the first makefile "fig3-9a.mk" and it will include everything through the make rule for pgm2. The remainder of Figure 3.9 will be a makefile called "fig3-9b.mk". The command:

```
$ make -f fig3-9.mk
```

is equivalent to the following command:

```
$ make -f fig3-9a.mk -f fig3-9b.mk
```

The important thing to understand is that the makefiles are concatenated before they are processed. Thus, it is as if they were one makefile. As we shall see in Chapter 6, this feature can be useful in the design of modular makefiles.

4.5.3 Using Standard Input to Get a "makefile"

Another feature of the **-f** option is the use of the minus sign, "-", as a valid file name. This variation causes **make** to read standard input for the makefile. For example, one could enter the following command:

```
$ cat fig3-9.mk | make -f -
```

While this example illustrates the concept, it is not very functional. However, it is possible to pipe the output of a preprocessor such as **vc** or **m4** (see Chapter 8) into the **make** command. Therefore, the following is also a valid form of the **make** command:

```
$ cat fig3-9b.mk | make -f fig3-9a.mk -f -
```

4.5.4 Retrieving a "makefile" from an SCCS File

Previously, we discussed the retrieval of a makefile from an SCCS file when **[mM]akefile** cannot be found. Similarly, **make** will look for **s.{makefile}** when the **-f** option is used and **{makefile}** cannot be found. In both cases, some implementations of **make** remove the retrieved makefile when **make** terminates processing.

While at first glance this feature seems somewhat limited, there are ways to make it more viable. **make** contains a list of default macro definitions, which includes the definitions for **${GET}** and **${GFLAGS}**. The default values for these macro definitions are as follows:

```
${GET}=get
${GFLAGS}=
```

By using either environmental variables or command line macro definitions, we could modify the definitions for these macros. But, as we shall see, modifying macros by either of these means has its consequences. Ignoring these consequences for the moment, the following command alters the version of the retrieved file:

```
$ GFLAGS=-r1.2 make
```

When searching for **s.[mM]akefile**, the **make** command assumes that the SCCS file exists in the current working directory. However, the price paid for building a software package in the SCCS source tree is loss of source file security.[4] Working in a secure software environment means that **s.[mM]akefile** would be located in the source library and not in the current working directory. But how can we communicate the SCCS path information to **make**?

We can maintain source file security while retrieving a source by using a special version of the **get** command. This new command will interface to the **get** command through an SUID Interface program.[5] However, if we execute the command:

```
$ GET=sget make
```

the **make** command will fail with the following message:

```
Make: No arguments or description file. Stop.
```

The problem is that **make** searches for the SCCS file before issuing the **${GET}** command. When the SCCS file cannot be found, **make** fails. To get past this behavior, we must use the **-g** option, which is an undocumented option of the **make** command. The **-g** option first searches for **{makefile}**. If the file is not found, the **${GET}** command is executed for **s.{makefile}** without first searching for **s.{makefile}** in the current working directory. Using the **-g** option, the command is as follows:

```
$ GET=sget make -g
```

The danger with using the **-g** option is that someone may decide to disable it since it is not documented. However, without this option, the ability of **make** to use SCCS files is a useless feature in a secure environment. We will visit this subject again in Chapter 5 when we discuss inference rules.

---

[4]Issues involving source file security are beyond the scope of this work. For those readers interested in more information, see Chapters 10 and 11 of Israel Silverberg, *Source File Management with SCCS* (Englewood Cliffs, N.J.: Prentice Hall, 1992).

[5]Both of these programs were described in Silverberg, *Source File Management with SCCS*. The **sget** command is described in Appendix F of this book, and Appendix D describes the SUID interface program.

4.6   Altering the Processing Parameters

Previously, we discussed the default processing parameters for the **make** command. Now we will discuss the options that change the operation of make and, in addition, how these options might be used.

4.6.1 Changing the Order of Precedence

The issue is the order of precedence in assigning definitions to macro names. Based on the preceding discussion of **make**, from highest priority to lowest priority, the default order of precedence is as follows:

1. *Macro definitions on* "make" *command line:* As mentioned in Section 4.3, command line processing occurs immediately after processing the **MAKEFLAGS** variable. Although they are the first to be processed, the command line macro definitions have the *highest precedence* and, therefore, will override any other definition for the macro name.

2. *Macro definition lines in the makefile:* From here on out, the order of precedence is the inverse of the order of processing. In other words, the last definition takes precedence over any previous definition. Since the macro definition lines are the last to be processed, these definitions override all definitions except command line macro definitions.

3. *Environmental variables:* Environmental variables play a dual role in that **make** treats them as macro definitions and as environmental variables. As environmental variables, the command lines inherit them when they are executed. For example, the following command lines produce equivalent results if **TEST** is an environmental variable:

```
exmpl :
    echo $$TEST    # TEST as a shell variable
    echo ${TEST}   # TEST as a macro
```

Again, since **TEST** is an environmental variable, the following command lines will also produce equivalent results:

```
TEST="internal definition"
exmpl :
    echo $$TEST    # TEST as a shell variable
    echo ${TEST}   # TEST as a macro
```

However, in this example, the value for **TEST** defined on the macro definition line takes precedence over the original value.

4. *Default macro definitions:* As we shall see in Chapter 5, there are many default macro definitions to use in writing **makefiles**. Since the makefile is appended to the internal descriptions, every form of explicit definition takes precedence.

Of the four ways to define macros, the first three can be considered **explicit macro definitions** since their value is not predetermined. Of these, the environmental variable has the lowest precedence in terms of explicit macro definitions.

How to use the order of precedence can be illustrated with the **PATH** variable. As an environmental variable, the **PATH** variable is read by **make** and passed to the command lines. However, if we wish to maintain strict control over the tools used to build a software package, we must control the **PATH** variable. By explicitly defining the **PATH** variable within the makefile, the makefile definition will override the definition received. Of course, when necessary, a command line macro definition could be used to override the value assigned in the makefile.

Instead of using the makefile to control the environment, we may want to have the environment control the makefile. This allows the establishment of a flexible environment without having to edit the makefile or having to enter all the macro definitions on the **make** command line. We can use the **-e** option to change the order of precedence so that environmental variables have a higher precedence than the macro definition lines.

Using the makefile defined previously, the following series of commands illustrates how to change the order of precedence:

```
$ TEST="environmental variable"; export TEST
$ make -e
```

Of course, command line macro definitions still take precedence over all other forms of macro definitions. To prove this, try the following series of commands:

```
$ TEST="environmental variable"; export TEST
$ make -e "TEST=command line macro"
```

4.6.2 Ignoring the Internal Description File

The **make** command has a built-in description file that includes macro definition lines, make rules, inference rules, and suffix rules (see Chapter 5 for a detailed discussion). In essence, **make** appends the makefile, an external description file, to the internal description file. By using the **-r** option, we can force **make** to use only the rules defined in the makefile. To illustrate the difference, the following command prints the internal description file plus environmental variables:

```
$ echo "" | make -p -f - 2> /dev/null | pg
```

With the following command, only the environmental variables will be listed:

```
$ echo "" | make -r -p -f - 2> /dev/null | pg
```

Using this option, it is possible to substitute another file for the internal description file. The trick is to use the **-f** option to concatenate multiple makefiles, as shown in the following example:

```
$ make -r -f new-default.mk -f [Mm]akefile
```

> **Warning!** The **-r** option will cause the **${GET}** and **${GFLAGS}** variables to have a null definition. As a result, **make** will not be able to execute the retrieval of a makefile from an SCCS file unless these variables are defined as environmental variables or command line macro definitions.

4.6.3 Ignoring Return Codes

As discussed in Section 3.3.4, **make** automatically terminates the processing of a makefile when the execution of a command line produces a nonzero return code. Whereas prefixing a command line with a "-" causes **make** to ignore the results of that line, the **-i** option causes **make** to ignore all command line return codes. This option is equivalent to the **.IGNORE** target (see Section 5.7).

> **Warning!** This option should be used with extreme care. To be on the safe side, it should only be used for debugging purposes. Any other use could result in the masking of errors in the final package.

4.6.4 Continue Processing after an Error

The **-k** option is a less drastic version of the **-i** option. Instead of totally ignoring nonzero return codes from the execution of command lines, the execution of the remaining command lines in the make rule is aborted. However, the execution of the makefile is not terminated.

The makefile shown in Figure 4.1 is used for this demonstration. To keep this makefile separate from other makefiles, let's call it fig4-1.mk. As an aid to help understand what is happening, Figure 4.2 shows the dependency tree for Figure 4.1.

If the command

```
$ make -f fig4-1.mk
```

is executed, the **make** command will end when it tries to make **tst1a** with the following messages:

```
tst1a - error return
*** Error code 1
Stop.
```

If the **-i** option is used, the error codes will be ignored and all the targets will be made. The only problem is that the building of **tst1**, **tst2**, **tst3**, and **test** is based on dependencies that have errors. Thus, ignoring the error codes has perpetuated the errors throughout the build process.

Now, lets see how the **-k** option works. The command

```
$ make -f fig4-1.mk -k
```

will produce the following output:

```
tst1a - error return
*** Error Code 1
tst1b - completed

tst2a - error return
*** Error Code 1

tst2b - completed
tst4 - completed
`test' not remade because of errors
```

```
test : tst1 tst2 tst3 tst4
       @echo "test target executed"

tst1 : tst1a tst1b
       @echo "tst1 - completed"

tst1a :
       @echo "tst1a - error return"; exit 1

tst1b :
       @echo "tst1b - completed"
tst2 : tst2a tst2b
       @echo "tst2 - completed"

tst2a :
       @echo "tst2a - error return"; exit 1
tst2b :
       @echo "tst2b - completed"

tst3 : tst1a tst2a
       @echo "tst3 - completed"

tst4 : tst1b tst2b
       @echo "tst4 - completed"
```

Figure 4.1 Demonstration for **-k** Option

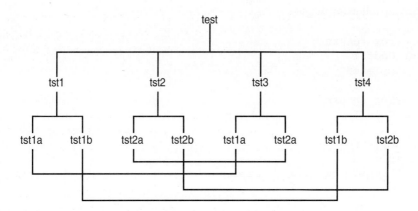

Figure 4.2 Dependency Tree for Figure 4.1

As can be seen, the building of **tst1a** and **tst2a** terminated. The error status was transmitted up the dependency tree and prevented the building of **tst1**, **tst2**, and **tst3**. Since these were not built, the building of **test** was blocked. However, those targets (**tst1b**, **tst2b**, and **tst4**) that were not related to **tst1a** and **tst2a** were built.

The **-k** option serves a useful purpose in the development environment. It allows us to find all the targets that have errors without allowing the errors to affect the final package object. The **-k** option is definitely much safer than the **-i** option.

4.6.5 Touch Targets

The **make** command normally executes the associated command lines when a target is older than any of its dependencies. With the **-t** option, **make** changes the modification time of each target to the current time. However, the command lines are not executed. Using Figure 3.9 as an example, the command:

```
$ make -t -f fig3-9.mk
```

will print the following information:

```
touch(moda.o)
touch(pgm1)
touch(modb.o)
touch(pgm2)
```

The targets will be marked as if they were made at the current time without executing any command lines. As a result, any changes to any dependencies will be totally
ignored. To prove this, execute the preceding command after executing the following
command:

```
$ touch mod[ab].c
```

> **Warning!** Careless use of this command can cause targets to be marked
> current that are not current.
>
> **Warning!** Touching a dummy target will result in the creation of a file
> name with the same name as the dummy target. If the dummy target
> has no dependencies (for example, the "clean" target in Figure 3.9), the
> target will always be considered as up to date and the command lines
> will never be executed.

4.6.6 Do Not Execute

The **-n** option gives a preview of which command lines will be executed. However, the command lines are not actually executed. This option is useful in the debugging of makefiles. For
example, the following command:

```
$ make -n -f fig3-9.mk
```

will produce the following output:

```
cc -c moda.c
cc -o pgm moda.o pgm1.c
cc -c modb.c
cc -o pgm2 moda.o modb.o pgm2.c
```

From this we can check the macro substitutions and the command lines. However,
we don't know what happened on the dependency lines. To check the dependency line
macro substitutions, we must use the **-p** option.

4.6.7 Backward Compatibility

The purpose of the **-b** option is to provide backward compatibility with "old" versions of
make. This flag is set by default. The question arises about the meaning of the phrase "an
old version of **make**." The first reference to this command appeared in the documentation
for UNIX System III. At that time, the documentation[6] included the additional comment
that "The difference between the old version of **make** and this version is that this version

---

[6]T. A. Dolotta, S. B. Olsson, A. G. Petrucelli, eds., *UNIX User's Manual: Release 3.0* (Murray Hill, N.J.: Bell
Telephone Laboratories, Inc., 1980), p. make.2.

requires all dependency lines to have a (possibly null) command associated with them. The previous version of **make** assumed if no command was specified explicitly that the command was null." It is the last sentence in this quotation that raises the question of whether the **-b** option continues to serve any real function. If one looks back at the examples presented in this book, there are many cases (for example, Figures 3.1, 3.9, and 4.1) of a dependency line with no associated command line. The implication is that the **-b** option is a vestigial element from the past.

4.6.8 Checking the Target

The **-q** option radically alters the functioning of the **make** command. The processing through the execution of the specified target(s) remains the same. After this point, the **-q** changes the purpose of **make**. Now, only the dependency lines are tested to see if the targets are up to date. If the target(s) are up to date, the return code is zero (0). If not, the return code is 255. The only output from the **-q** option is the return code. If you want to see the effect of this option, enter the following commands:

```
$ make -f fig3-9.mk   # will make everything current
$ make -f fig3-9.mk -q all; echo $?
0
$ touch modb.c   # make modb.c out-of-date
$ make -f fig3-9.mk -q pgm1; echo $?
0
$ make -f fig3-9.mk -q pgm2; echo $?
255
$ make -f fig3-9.mk -q -k pgm1 pgm2; echo $?
255
```

As you can see, the **-q** option only checks the status of a target. If the target is up to date, the return code is 0. When checking multiple targets, the **-k** option is needed on some versions of **make** to ensure that the entire makefile is checked. Should any target be out of date, or if there is an error, the return code is 255. Also, a dummy target that has no dependencies, such as "clean", would always be considered out of date. Since only the dependency line is used, the following is also a valid form of the command:

```
$ echo "pgm1 : pgm1.c" | make -f - -q; echo $?
```

This format allows one to compare the modification time of any target name against the modification time of one or more dependency names.

4.7   Altering the Output

Besides any warning or error messages, the **make** command always prints the command line before it is executed. The following sections discuss how to expand or suppress the amount of information printed.

4.7.1 Verbose Print

The **-p** option prints a long list of information that defines the environment for **make** at the point that **make** starts processing the first target. As a result, this listing precedes the normal output from **make** and contains output from both standard output and standard error.

The information written to standard output is useful for debugging and is composed of the following sections:

1. Information from the **get** command when the makefile was retrieved from an SCCS File.

2. A list of the macro definitions.

3. A list of the make rules in inverse order and with the macros in the dependency line expanded.

4. A list of the default make rules.

5. A list of the default inference rules.

6. The definition for the special target .SUFFIXES (see Chapter 5 for more details).

Since the output of the **-p** option is rather lengthy, you can use one of the following two forms of the command:

```
$ make -f fig3-9.mk -p 1> plst 2> elst
$ make -f fig3-9.mk -p 2> /dev/null | pg
```

In both commands, we split standard error from standard output. In the first command, standard error is directed to the file **elst** and standard output is directed to **plst**. In the second example, standard error is ignored and standard output is piped to **pg** or, if available, **more**. Splitting standard error from standard output is not the desired alternative, since standard error contains descriptive tags that are important. Unfortunately, the two outputs are only in sync when the output is directed to the terminal, which is a character device. When directed to a block device, the two streams are out of sync because merging the two streams of characters is done in blocks.

You will notice that the **-p** option does not provide any additional information regarding the processing of the make rules. The information for processing the targets was previously provided by the **-d** and **-m** options, which seem to have disappeared between UNIX System III and UNIX System V.

4.7.2 Suppress Printing of Command Lines

By using the **-s** option, it is possible to run in a silent mode. This will suppress the printing of the command lines on standard output, leaving only the error messages to be printed on standard error. However, the **-i**, **-k**, and **-p** options override the **-s** option and the command lines are printed. This option has the same effect as the **".SILENT"** (see Section 5.7).

4.8   Environmental Variables as Macros

Environmental variables play a dual role in the processing of makefiles. In this section, our discussion looks at the environmental variables inherited by **make** and how they can be used and modified. First, we discuss how to define an environmental variable and then how to define a macro. Finally, we discuss how the two are used. The importance of this section will become more apparent as we learn more about creating a hierarchical structure of makefiles.

4.8.1 Defining an Environmental Variable

There are three ways to define an environmental variable:

1. *By exporting it to the environment:* In the Bourne shell, this would be accomplished as follows:

```
$ EVAR="this is a variable"; export EVAR
```

For C Shell users, the syntax is slightly different:

```
% setenv EVAR this is a variable
```

2. *By defining it on the command line:* It is also possible to define an environmental variable on the **make** command line, as shown in the following example:

```
$ EVAR="this is a variable" make
```

The difference between this method of defining an environmental variable and the previous method is one of scope. When defined on the command line, the variable is only part of the environment during the execution of the remaining commands on the line and does not become part of the login shell's environment.

3. *By using a command line macro definition:* If environmental variables generate macro definitions and command line macro definitions generate environmental variables, what is the difference? Simply, command line macro definitions have a higher precedence than environmental variables. As the following example shows, the difference in syntax between a command line macro definition and the definition of an environmental variable is position on the command line:

```
$ make EVAR="this is a test"
```

You can also use the command line macro definition as a selective version of the **-e** option. With the e option, all environmental variables take precedence over macro definition lines. By using command line macro definitions, only selected variables take precedence.

4.8.2 Defining a Macro

Besides the default macro definitions, there are only three ways to define a macro. In the normal order of ascending precedence, these are as follows (for the exception to this, see the **-e** option):

1. *Environmental variables:* Every environmental variable is automatically defined as a macro.

2. *Macro definition lines:* The normal operation of **make** allows the macro definition line to assert positive control over the definition of macros. However, if the **-e** option is used, the role of the macro definition line changes to providing the default definition. With the **-e** option, positive control was transferred from the macro definition line to the environmental variable. For example, under normal operation, the environmental variable sets the default value for **PATH**, and the macro definition line can override this definition. With the **-e** option, the macro definition line defines the default value and the environmental variable overrides.

3. *Command line macro definitions:* The command line macro definition provides the other means of creating a macro definition. Owing to its priority in the order of precedence, it will override all other macro definitions.

4.8.3 Using Environmental Variables and Macros

The difference between an environmental variable and a macro definition is one of scope of impact. The macro definition only affects the makefile being currently processed. For example, a macro definition replaces a macro name on a command line, whereas the environmental variable is inherited by the shell when a command line is executed. If the command line contains another **make** command (see Recursive Makefiles in Section 6.3), then the environmental variable provides a vehicle for passing information from one makefile to another.

> **Note:** A macro definition line may change an environmental variable, but it cannot create one. An environmental variable must be defined before processing a makefile.

4.9 Summary

In Chapter 3, we learned how to write a simple makefile using explicit target names. In this chapter, we learned how **make** will process that makefile. Of the many topics discussed in this chapter, certain topics must be understood. Without implying an order of importance, these topics are as follows:

1. *Environmental variables:* Except for **MAKEFLAGS**, the environment received by **make** is passed to the command line environment. Macro definition lines may change an environmental variable, but they cannot create one.

2. *Precedence of macro definitions*: With the default order of precedence, the macro definition lines in the makefile take precedence. By using the **-e** option, the environment variable takes precedence. However, the command line macro definition always takes precedence over macro definition lines and environmental variables.

3. *Changing names for the description file:* Although the default makefile names usually suffice, the **-f** option allows us to use a different name or to concatenate makefiles. The **-g** option, although not documented, provides an important interface to SCCS.

4. *Selection of target names:* Most makefiles contain more than one make rule. By specifying the target name on the **make** command line, we tell **make** which target to process. When a target name does not appear on the **make** command line, the first explicit make rule found is processed.

With this information, we are ready to tackle the writing of more advanced makefiles. This will be the subject of Chapter 5.

CHAPTER 5

Writing Advanced "makefiles"

5.1   Introduction

Although they may be a little long and cumbersome, the makefiles developed from the information presented in the last two chapters solve most problems. The material presented in this chapter will simplify and add more flexibility to these basic makefiles. Upon completion of this chapter, we will be ready to discuss how makefiles can be implemented in a production environment.

5.2   More on the Dependency Line

In Chapter 3, we covered the common rules for the dependency line. In this section, we cover the rules for some features that are less commonly used. However, when needed, they can greatly simplify a makefile.

Until now, our examples limited the target name to one dependency line. In addition, only the single colon separated the target from the dependency names on the dependency line. However, it is possible to use the same target name on more than one dependency line. The difference between single and double colons only has meaning in this situation. This difference is best explained by looking at the following contexts.

5.2.1 Multiple Targets with Shared Dependencies

What happens when two or more make rules have the same set of command lines but with variations in dependency names? What difference does it make if we have a few extra make rules in a makefile? Why should we bother trying to reduce the number of make rules to a minimum? If you think of a set of command lines as a source module, then the reasons for minimizing duplication become more apparent. Just as the use of common source modules reduces the effort required in writing, changing, and debugging a module, so does the use of a common set of command lines.

Figure 5.1 shows an example in which the only difference between the two make rules is the dependency names referring to include files. For the purposes of this discussion, the term *include files* encompasses source files merged into a primary source file via a preprocessor (the **cpp** command for 'C') or as part of the language syntax (the COBOL COPY statement). Thus, the include file may not alter the command line, but does affect the dependency line.

```
all : pgm1a pgm2a

pgm1a : $$@.c exmpl1.h
        cc -o $@ $@.c

pgm2a : $$@.c exmpl2.h
        cc -o $@ $@.c

clean :
        -rm -f pgm1a pgm2a
```

Figure 5.1 Example of Duplicate Command Linesm

```
all : pgm1a pgm2a

pgm1a : exmpl1.h

pgm2a : exmpl2.h

pgm1a pgm2a : $$@.c
        cc -o $@ $@.c

clean :
        -rm -f pgm1a pgm2a
```

Figure 5.2 Multiple Targets with Shared Dependencies

The makefile shown in Figure 5.1 can be rewritten as shown in Figure 5.2. Notice that, by using a single colon on each dependency line, it is possible to concatenate all the dependency lines related to a single target name.

> **Note:** The order of the dependency lines is not important. They also need not be grouped together. However, only one dependency line is allowed to have any associated command lines.

5.2.2 Multiple Targets with Shared Command Lines

In Section 5.2.1, our objective was to create a single set of command lines for different dependencies. We are now going to concatenate multiple make rules into a single make rule when the target is processed. As before, the purpose for this exercise is to reduce the occurrence of like command lines.

```
# An Example of a Simple Makefile Using Double Colons
MODA = moda
MODB = modb
OBJS = ${MODA}.o ${MODB}.o
PGMS = pgm1 pgm2
POBJS = pgm1.o pgm2.o
LIBS = -lc

all : ${PGMS}

${PGMS} :: $$@.c
        cc -c $@.c

pgm1 :: ${MODA}.o
        ld -o $@ ${MODA}.o $@.o ${LIBS}

pgm2 :: ${OBJS}
        ld -o $@ ${OBJS} $@.o ${LIBS}

${PGMS} ::
        @echo "Build of $@ was successful"

${MODA}.o : ${MODA}.c
        cc -c ${MODA}.c

${MODB}.o : ${MODB}.c
        cc -c ${MODB}.c
```

Figure 5.3 Example makefile using Double Colons

```
clean :
        -rm -f ${OBJS} ${POBJS} ${PGMS}
        @echo "work files removed"
```

Figure 5.3 Example makefile using Double Colons (Continued)

The makefile shown in Figure 5.3, which is a modified version of the one shown in Figure 3.9, illustrates how this feature of **make** works. In this example, we divided the making of **pgm1** and **pgm2** into two common make rules (rules 1 and 4) and two independent make rules (rules 2 and 3). From this example, we can make the following observations:

1. The **double colon** defines a particular make rule as a member of a set of make rules.

2. Dependencies belong to a particular make rule. Thus, whereas all the targets with the same name are checked, only those that are out of date are made. By executing the following commands, we can see how this works:

```
$ touch moda.c
```

```
$ make -f fig5-3.mk
```

3. The make rules are executed in the order in which they occur. However, they do not need to be consecutive.

Using dependencies to solve a problem when the double colon would have been a better solution is a common mistake. For example, the double colons in Figure 5.3 could be replaced by the following:

```
all : pgm1 pgm
        @echo "Build of $? was successful"

pgm1 : $$@.o ${MODA}.o
        ld -o $@ ${MODA}.o $@.o ${LIBS}

pgm2 : $$@.o ${OBJS}
        ld -o $@ ${OBJS} $@.o ${LIBS}
```

In this example, a default inference rule (see Section 5.4) handles the compilation of the program. Although both solutions work, the double colon solution presents a more accurate reflection of the problem that we are trying to solve. Whenever we have common command lines that can be shared, we should use double colons.

5.3 More on Macro Definitions

Up to now, we have been dealing with a very simple makefile in a very simple environment. While still maintaining a simple makefile, we will begin to complicate the environment. Instead of building the package objects in the current working directory, we will build them in an object directory called **$HOME/pkgobj**. In addition, we are going to add a little source file control by having the source files be dependent on their corresponding SCCS files. Furthermore, these SCCS files will not be located in the current working directory, but in the source library. Finally, we will convert the tools used to standard naming conventions. All this will be done through the use a few additional macro features of **make**. The result of this effort is shown in Figure 5.4.

```
Note: The line numbers are for reference purposes only

 1  # An Example of a Simple Makefile Using More Macros
 2  RM = rm
 3  LIBS = -lc
 4  SLIB = /srclib/exmpl
 5  PKGOBJ = ${HOME}/pkgobj
 6  MODA = moda
 7  MODB = modb
 8  OBJS = moda.o modb.o
 9  PGMS = ${PKGOBJ}/pgm1 ${PKGOBJ}/pgm2
10  POBJ = pgm1.o pgm2.o
11
12  all : ${PGMS}
13
14  ${PGMS} :: $$(@F).c
15          ${CC} ${CFLAGS} -c ${@F}.c
16
17  ${PKGOBJ}/pgm1 :: ${MODA}.o
18          ${LD} ${LDFLAGS} -o $@ ${MODA}.o ${@F}.o ${LIBS}
19
20  ${PKGOBJ}/pgm2 :: ${OBJS}
21          ${LD} ${LDFLAGS} -o $@ ${OBJS} ${@F}.o ${LIBS}
22
23  ${PGMS} ::
24          @echo "Build of ${@F} in directory ${@D} completed."
25
26  ${OBJS} : ${OBJS:.o=.c}
27          ${CC} ${CFLAGS} -c ${@:.o=.c}
```

Figure 5.4 Makefile Using More Macros

```
28
29   ${POBJ:.o=.c} ${OBJS:.o=.c} : ${SLIB}/s.$$@
30           ${GET} ${GFLAGS} ${SLIB}/s.$@
31
32   clean :
33           -${RM} -f ${OBJS} ${POBJ} ${PGMS}
34           @echo "work files removed"
```

Figure 5.4 Makefile Using More Macros (Continued)

5.3.1 More on Internal Macros

In Chapter 3, we discussed the **$@** and **$?** internal macros because they are used with explicit make rules. In addition, there are two other internal macros (**$*** and **$<**) that can only be used with inference rules and one internal macro (**$%**) that is used only when dealing with archive libraries. Table 5.1 describes each of these internal macros and the rules for their use. A more detailed description of the **$*** and **$<** internal macros is found in Section 5.4. The **$%** internal macro is discussed in Section 5.6.

Table 5.1   Description of Internal Macros

Macro	Definition	Limitations
$@	Current full target name {base name}{to suffix}	Explicit rule or inference rule target.
$$@	Current full target name	Explicit rule only. The $$@ is used as a dependency name. The macro supports both the F and D suffixes but not macro substitution.
$?	Out-of-date dependency list	Explicit rule and only on command line.
$%	Member name of library when the target has the format *library(member)*	Explicit rule or inference rule. The $@ can be used to determine the library name. The F and D suffixes are not allowed.
$*	{base name} of target without suffix	Inference rule.
$<	{base name}{from suffix}	Inference rule. Refers to the dependency name.

As discussed in Chapter 1, the SCCS source tree, the work source tree, and the package image tree must be kept separate. This means that some target names will include the full path name for the target. For example, in Figure 5.4, the path name for **pgm1** is **${PKGOBJ}** and the target name is **${PKGOBJ}/${PGM1}**, which is the value assigned to the $@ macro.

Because this places the package object in the package image tree, it creates a problem when trying to reference the corresponding object and source files. The make command provides two modifiers to all internal macros (except for $%) that solve this problem. These modifiers are 'D' for the directory portion of the target name and 'F' for the file name portion. Using the preceding example, **${@D}** refers to **${PKGOBJ}** and **${@F}** refers to **${PGM1}**. Lines 14, 15, 18, 21, and 24 of Figure 5.4 show various uses of the **D** and **F** modifiers.

> **Note!** Adding the suffix to the internal macro changes the macro from a single-character macro to a multiple-character macro. Thus, there is a big difference between **$@F**, which evaluates to **{target name}F**, and **${@F}**, which defines the file name portion of the target name.

> **Warning!** When either **D** or **F** qualify an internal macro on the dependency line, *parentheses must be used as delimiters*, not braces. Some implementations of **make** incorrectly parse the internal macro **$${@F}**. To check how your version of **make** behaves, execute a makefile that uses a qualified internal macro on a dependency line. The output produced from **make -p** must show the internal macro as $(@F) or ${@F}. Any other value (for example, just the '$' appears without the rest of the macro) indicates that the internal macro was not correctly processed.

The documentation for UNIX System V[1] says that the **$?** macro is excluded from using the 'D' and 'F' suffixes. *This is not true for all implementations of* **make**. The **${?D}** macro will produce a list of directories that are out of date and the **${?F}** will produce a list of files that are out of date. However, the suffixes do not apply to the **$%** macro since it references a module name within a library (see Section 5.6).

5.3.2 Macro String Substitution

The **make** command provides a limited means of modifying the macro definition via string substitution. The format for defining the substitution string is:

[1]AT&T, *UNIX System V: Programmer's Reference Manual* (Englewood Cliffs, N.J.: Prentice Hall, 1987), p. 74.

```
$({macro name}:{subst1}=[{subst2}])
```

where **{subst1}** is interpreted according to the following:

```
.*{subst1}[space|tab|new-line]²
```

From the delimiting characters used in **{subst1}**, we can see that changing suffixes is the only use for macro string substitution. While **{subst1}** must define a suffix string of the macro definition, **{subst2}** can be any valid string. As a corollary, if **{subst2}** is not specified, it is defined as **null,** thereby providing a means to delete a suffix. From the following examples, we see that the **{macro name}** can refer to either explicit macro definitions or to internal macros:

```
${MODA:.o=.c}
${@:.o=.c}
${@F:.sh=}
```

Usually, macro substitution strings can be used on macro definition lines, dependency lines, and command lines (see lines 26, 27, and 29 in Figure 5.4). However, in a few cases, macro substitution does not lead to the correct result. For example, the following makefile results in the target names remaining as macros (you can use **make -p** to verify the results):

```
PGM1=pgm1
OBJS=${PGM1}.o

${OBJS:.o=.c} : s.$$@
       get s.$@
```

After processing the macro substitution, the target name is **${PGM1}.c**. For some reason, **make** does not do another pass of the target name to resolve any remaining macros. As a result, our example target name remains a macro. However, the following makefile will work correctly:

```
OBJS=pgm1.o

${OBJS:.o=.c} : s.$$@
       get s.$@
```

---

[2]AT&T, *UNIX System V: Programmer's Reference Manual*, p. 73 states that the beginning of a line is also a delimiter, but this is not the case. The substitution format is the form shown in AT&T, *Unix System V: Programmer's Guide* (Englewood Cliffs, N.J.: Prentice Hall, 1987), p. 638.

> **Warning!** Macro string substitution for the $$@ macro does not work on dependency lines. While the macro $${@:.o=.c} is correctly processed on the first pass, it is incorrectly evaluated on the next pass.

Because of the problem of macro substitution in dependencies, line 26 in Figure 5.4 is not actually correct. The correct dependency should be $${@:.o=.c}. As it is written, any change in moda.c or modb.c results in the recompilation of both moda.o and modb.o. Our discussion of inference rules presents a better solution to this problem.

5.3.3 More on Default Macros

In Chapter 4, we discussed the **${GET}** and **${GFLAGS}** default macros. These two macros are part of a larger set of macro definitions for the common commands and their related options. Figure 5.5 lists the predefined macros that are present in UNIX System V Release 3. You can easily see which default macros are available on your system with the following command:

```
$ echo "" | make -p -f - 2> /dev/null | pg
```

The first macros listed will be environmental variables. After the environmental variables, the default macros are listed. You can see that most commands are represented by a pair of macro definitions; one macro defines the command and one macro defines the options.

> **Recommendation!** The use of macros for commands and their arguments should be practiced throughout the makefile. If a predefined macro does not exist, define a new pair. These new definitions can be kept in a standard include file (see Section 5.5) that can then be included in every makefile.

```
ARFLAGS = rv
AR = ar

ASFLAGS =
AS = as

CFLAGS = -O
CC = cc

F77FLAGS =
F77 = f77

GFLAGS =
GET = get

LDFLAGS =
LD = ld

LFLAGS =
LEX = lex

MAKEFLAGS = b  (value is determined by flags on command line)
MAKE = make

YFLAGS =
YACC = yacc
```

Figure 5.5 Predefined Macros for Makefile

5.4   Inference Rules

As shown in the examples we have used, the make rules define a series of stages for building a package object. Thus, a 'C' program is compiled to create an object file, and the object
files are linked together to form an executable object. Although limited to the definition of
${PGM_NAME}, the following make rule describes how the compilation of a 'C' program
creates an object file:

```
${PGM_NAME}.o : $$@.c
        ${CC} ${CFLAGS} -c $@.c
```

This hypothetical make rule *transforms* any 'C' file into an object file. Rather than
always having to define ${PGM_NAME}, we need a way to write generic rules. The

make command provides the means for writing a generic make rule, which is called an **inference rule.**[3]

The idea behind the inference rule is based on the suffixes used to identify each type of UNIX file. Simply stated, an inference rule is a make rule with a special dependency line and a few special internal macros to reference this special dependency line. The following sections describe how an inference rule works in more detail. Appendix A lists the default inference rules that are common to **make**.

5.4.1 Suffixes: The Key

Without thinking, we know that a file ending in ".c" is a 'C' program, a file ending in ".o" is an object file, and a file with no suffix is probably an executable file. This idea of using suffixes to identify the type of file is so ingrained into the soul of a programmer that the suffix becomes the name for the type of file. We can speak of ".c", ".h", or ".o" files and everyone knows what we are talking about. Table 5.2 lists the suffixes that are commonly recognized by **make**. To find out which suffixes are supported on your version of **make,** see Section 5.4.3.

With suffixes being such an integral part of the method of file identification, it is only natural to use suffixes to identify the inference rule. The following defines the **target name** (the name that identifies a make rule) for an inference rule:

```
{from suffix}{to suffix}
```

For example, the target name for an inference rule that transforms a ".c" file to an ".o" file would be ".c.o". From the target name we know that we are transforming a 'C' source file into an object file. Since the target name for an inference rule is a special name that carries additional meaning, we will call it an **inference target**.

When dealing with suffixes, it is important to remember that the **base name** (the name without the suffix) remains constant throughout the transformation process. So, what we are talking about is the transformation of the file **{base name}{from suffix}** to the file **{base name}{to suffix}**. For example, when we compile a program, we transform *pgm1.c* to *pgm1.o*.

5.4.2 The Tilde: A Link to SCCS

There is one common context in which a file is identified by its prefix and not by its suffix; this is the SCCS file. Since the suffix identifies the type of file, an SCCS file is prefixed with "s.". Therefore, the file name **s.pgm1.c** says that this is the SCCS file of the 'C' source file for pgm1.

---

[3]AT&T, *UNIX System V: Programmer's Guide*, p. 640, refers to inference rules as **transformation** rules. Although the term is more descriptive of the actual process, we will use the term **inference rule** since this is the term used in AT&T, *UNIX System V: Programmer's Reference Manual*, p. 75.

When we use SCCS to manage source files, how do we establish a relationship between the SCCS file and the source file? The solution used by **make** is to suffix the suffix with a tilde (~). For example, if ".c" identifies a 'C' source file, then ".c~" identifies the SCCS file for that same 'C' source file. Therefore, the target name for retrieving a source file from an SCCS file would be ".c~.c".

Table 5.2 Standard Suffixes

Suffix	Description
.a	Archive library
.c	**C** program source file
.f	FORTRAN source file
.h	Header file
.l	**'lex'** source file
.o	Object file
.s	Assembler source file
.sh	Shell file
.y	**'yacc'** source file

Note: The implicit assumption is that the SCCS file resides in the same directory as the corresponding source file. In addition, the default is to retrieve the version of the SCCS file that fulfills the condition of **mR.mL** (maximum Release Number and maximum Level Number within that Release Number). While other parameters can be provided via the **${GFLAGS}** macro, those parameters must apply to all executions of the **${GET}** command within the makefile.

Warning! Use of the tilde applies only to retrieving a source file from an SCCS file. It *does not* apply to storing a source file in an SCCS file, which depends on the **p-file** and not the SCCS file. More accurately, it depends on a record in the **p-file** and not on the **p-file** itself.[a]

[a] This occurs because the **p-file** serves as the link between the **get** command and the delta command. The relationship becomes complicated when several people may be working with the same SCCS file. For more information on this problem, see AT&T, *UNIX System V: Programmer's Guide*, p.682.

5.4.3 From Dependency to Inference Target

Now that we know how to use suffixes to define an inference target, we need to look at the implications of this new kind of target in more detail. With an explicit target name, the link between dependency name and target name is defined by an exact match of names. For example, the dependency name "moda.o" in line 17 of Figure 5.4 matches the target name in line 26. However, with the inference target, the link is not so obvious. Even within the list of default suffixes shown in Table 5.2, one can see that an object file can be derived from a 'C' source file, a FORTRAN source file, or an assembler source file. How does **make** know which source file to use? After all, as shown in Appendix A, there are inference targets for ".c.o", ".f.o", ".s.o", and so on.

The system used by make relies on a suffix list of potential {from suffix}s. This list is identified by the special target called ".SUFFIXES". Although there are implementation variations, the default ".SUFFIXES" should be similar to the following:

```
.SUFFIXES: .o .c .c~ .y .y~ .l .l~ .s .s~ .h .h~ .sh .sh~ .f .f~
```

To understand the search sequence of **make**, you need to read this suffix list from left to right. However, it must also be read in light of the inference rules that have been defined in the makefile and in the default description file. After all, not every suffix pair in the list will necessarily have a corresponding inference rule. To decide what rule to use, **make** looks for a file that has the name **{base name}{from suffix},** starting at the beginning of the suffix list and continuing until there is a matching inference rule for **{from suffix}{to suffix}**. Once a match is found, that inference rule is used.

However, this is not the end of the search. In actuality, the inference target is an abbreviated form of a dependency line in which the **{to suffix}** represents the **target name** and the **{from suffix}** represents the **dependency name**. Just as with any other dependency name, **make** first checks to see if there is an explicit target for this dependency and then checks for an inference rule. This cycle continues until there is no explicit target, inference rule, or file name that matches an inference rule.

A critical difference between explicit rules and inference rules revolves around how rules are chained together. Explicit rules will continue to check the dependencies to a target, although a file name for the particular dependency does not exist, whereas, for inference rules, a file name must exist for the **{base name}{from suffix}** combination.

Using Figure 5.4 as an example, if we are trying to make moda.o and moda.c does not exist, **make** will not search for a way to build the target. This happens even though there is a rule for making moda.c from an SCCS file. In terms of inference rules, the lack of moda.c would not automatically invoke the rule for ".c~.c". To solve this problem, we use the ".c~.o" inference rule. Once moda.c is created, the order of evaluation of inference rules will be ".c.o" and then ".c~.c". This order occurs because **.c** comes before **.c~** in the suffix list.

5.4.4 Changing the Suffix List

Whether to add new suffixes, delete existing suffixes, or change the order of precedence, the **.SUFFIXES** target does not follow the normal modification rules. The **.SUFFIXES** target only has two modes of operation: *add* suffixes to list and *delete* the entire suffix list. Thus, to change the existing suffix list, it must first be deleted and then a new suffix list added.

For example:

```
SUFFIXES : .p .p~
```

would add the new suffixes for PASCAL to the end of the default suffix list, whereas

```
SUFFIXES :
```

would delete the entire suffix list. By using both lines, we could create a new suffix list as follows:

```
.SUFFIXES :
.SUFFIXES : .o .p .p~
```

When adding to a suffix list or creating a new suffix list, remember that the order of the suffixes is important, because the order of the suffix list decides the order in which the inference rules are applied.

5.4.5 NULL Suffix

Up to this point, we have only discussed suffix pairs. Yet, if we were to write an inference rule to create an executable package object, we would have a problem since an executable package object does not usually have a suffix. This problem is solved by having a special **{to suffix}** that is called a **NULL suffix**. The latter part of Appendix A shows several examples in which the **{to suffix}** is a NULL suffix.

> **Note:** The **{from suffix}** can never be defined as a **NULL suffix**.

5.4.6 Command Lines for Inference Rules

The only difference between the command lines for an inference rule and those for an explicit make rule is the availability of additional internal macros. Besides the **$@** macro, the $* macro and the $< macro can be used. The meanings of these macros when used in inference rules are as follows:

```
$@       Refers to {base name}{to suffix}, which is the
         actual "target name."

$<       Refers to {base name}{from suffix}, which is the
         actual "dependency name."

$*       Refers to just the {base name}.
```

Just as the name for an explicit target may consist of both a file name and a path name, the **{base name}** may contain both elements. As a result, the **F** and **D** suffixes can be used to identify the file-name portion and the path-name portion.

5.4.7 Guidelines for Writing Inference Rules

Whether an inference rule is replaced or a new one added, the following should make the job a little easier.

1. An inference rule in the **makefile** replaces a default inference rule (see Appendix A for a list of the common default inference rules).

2. When adding an inference rule, make sure that the suffix list is correct. If the suffix list is not correct, use the **.SUFFIXES** target to make the necessary changes.

3. An inference rule can have *only one dependency*, the **{from suffix}**, and it must exist in the *same directory* as the target, the **{to suffix}**. This is a serious limitation when we consider that the work directory, SCCS directory, and package image directory may be different directories.

4. Dependencies other than **{base name}{from suffix}** can be placed on separate dependency lines. For example, the following would define the dependency for an include file:

```
pgm1.c : mypgm.h
.c.o :
          ${CC} ${CFLAGS} -c $<
```

Figure 5.6 shows how the **makefile** in Figure 5.4 can be modified to use inference rules. The inference rule for **.c.o** while not necessary, shows how to write an inference rule. The new inference rule overrides the equivalent default inference rule. Also, you will notice the use of an explicit make rule for the retrieval of a source file from an SCCS file. Although an inference rule would better serve the purpose, especially in a large makefile, we are trapped by the limitation described in point 3 above.

5.4.8 Disabling a Default Rule

As described in Chapter 4, the **-r** option to the **make** command ignores the default description file. However, there are times when we wish to disable a particular default inference rule. For example, we want only explicit rules to be used for compiling a program and, when such a rule does not exist, we want **make** to fail. In such cases, we can disable a single rule by including the following inference rule in our makefile:

```
{from suffix}{to suffix} :;
```

This is nothing more than a single-line make rule (see Chapter 3 for the complete format) with no command lines.

5.5   Include Files

In Chapter 4, we saw how we could use the **-f** option of the **make** command to concatenate several makefiles into one. Another way of bringing together several pieces to create one makefile is by using the **include line** in a makefile. The format is simply:

```
include {file name}
```

The word **include** must be the first word on a line and must be separated from the **{file name}** by a space or a tab. The **{file name}** may be defined by a macro name. For example:

```
include fig5-7a.mi
```

or

```
INC1 = fig5-7a.mi
include ${INC1}
```

are equivalent. The latter can be very useful when writing one makefile to serve different environments (such as building a software package for different machines) without having to modify the makefile.

To show how include files can be used, Figure 5.7 is a modified version of Figure 5.6. The missing lines are now part of the referenced include files. From this we can see that some uses of the include line are as follows:

```
# An Example of a Simple Makefile Using Inference Rules
RM = rm
LIBS = -lc
SLIB = /srclib/exmpl
PKGOBJ = ${HOME}/pkgobj
MODA = moda
MODB = modb
OBJS = moda.o modb.o
PGMS = ${PKGOBJ}/pgm1 ${PKGOBJ}/pgm2
POBJ = pgm1.o pgm2.o

all : ${PGMS}

${PKGOBJ}/pgm1 :: $$(@F).o ${MODA}.o
        ${LD} ${LDFLAGS} -o $@ ${MODA}.o ${@F}.o ${LIBS}

${PKGOBJ}/pgm2 :: $$(@F).o ${OBJS}
        ${LD} ${LDFLAGS} -o $@ ${OBJS} ${@F}.o ${LIBS}

${PGMS} ::
        @echo "Build of ${@F} in directory ${@D} completed."

.c.o :
        @echo "using new .c.o rule"
        ${CC} ${CFLAGS} -c $<

${POBJ:.o=.c} ${OBJS:.o=.c} : ${SLIB}/s.$$@
        ${GET} ${GFLAGS} ${SLIB}/s.$@

clean :
        -rm -f ${OBJS} ${POBJ}
        @echo "work files removed"
```

Figure 5.6 Example Makefile Using Inference Rules

1. Macro definitions that are common to more than one makefile can be incorporated into an include file. This is the standard means of incorporating system-wide definitions into each makefile without having to pass them as environmental variables or command line macros.

2. Inference rules that are common to more than one makefile can be incorporated into an include file.

3. Also, command lines can be put into an include file. This is a handy means of handling common routines.

Although not shown in the example, it is possible for an include file to contain include lines. Even though it would be confusing to read, including other include files can be continued for 16 levels.

5.6   Interface to Archive Libraries

In this section, we will discuss the special features of **make** that are related to archive libraries. The complete subject of the creation and maintenance of archive libraries is discussed in Chapter 11. For now, all we need to know is that an archive library is a file that contains other files called members. Furthermore, the member of the archive library is the subject of concern, not the library itself. Let's see how this works by first looking at the dependency line.

5.6.1 Dependency Line for an Archive Library

To reference a member of an archive library, the following format is used:

```
library(member)
```

Thus, if **moda.o** and **modb.o** were members of an archive library called **libex**, the following would be valid references to the members:

```
libex.a(moda.o)
libex.a(modb.o)
```

Or we could use a macro for the library name with the following results:

```
EX = libex.a
$(EX)(moda.o)
$(EX)(modb.o)
```

Notice that the $ prefix is all that is used to differentiate a **macro name** from a **member name**. A clearer separation of the two names can be obtained by using {} for **macro names**. Using this convention, the preceding lines would be as follows:

```
${EX}(moda.o)
${EX}(modb.o)
```

```
# An Example of a Simple Makefile Using the Include Line

include fig5-7a.mi
MODA = moda
MODB = modb
OBJS = moda.o modb.o
PGMS = ${PKGOBJ}/pgm1 ${PKGOBJ}/pgm2
POBJ = pgm1.o pgm2.o

all : ${PGMS}

${PKGOBJ}/pgm1 :: $$(@F).o ${MODA}.o
        ${LD} ${LDFLAGS} -o $@ ${MODA}.o ${@F}.o ${LIBS}

${PKGOBJ}/pgm2 :: $$(@F).o ${OBJS}
        ${LD} ${LDFLAGS} -o $@ ${OBJS} ${@F}.o ${LIBS}

${PGMS} ::
        @echo "Build of ${@F} in directory ${@D} completed."

include fig5-7b.mi

${POBJ:.o=.c} ${OBJS:.o=.c} : ${SLIB}/s.$$@
include fig5-7c.mi

clean :
        -rm -f ${OBJS} ${POBJ}
        @echo "work files removed"
```

Figure 5.7 Examples of How to Use the Include Line

The member name can be used as a dependency name. For example, to define the members of an archive library, the following dependency line would be used:

libex.a : libex.a(moda.o) libex.a(modb.o)

The member name can also be used as a target name as follows:

libex.a(moda.o) : moda.c

5.6.2 Internal Macros and Archive Libraries

The meanings of the internal macros are slightly different when dealing with archive libraries. These differences are as follows:

1. When a member name is used as a dependency name, the **$?** macro will give a list of the members that are out of date. However, this list will not include a reference to the library name.

2. When a member name is used as a target name, the **$@** macro will refer to the name of the archive library and the **$%** macro will refer to the name of the member within the archive library. The following example shows how this could be used:

```
libex.a(moda.o) : moda.
    ${CC} -c ${CFLAGS} ${%:.o=.c
    ${AR} ${ARFLAGS} $@ $%.
```

3. The internal macros used in inference rules have also changed. The **$@** macro refers to the name of the archive library and the **$*** macro refers to the member name without the suffix. The **$<** macro is the member name plus the **{from suffix}**.

5.6.3 Inference Rules and Archive Libraries

The most important difference between a regular inference rule and an inference rule for an archive library is that the suffix is for the library (**.a**) and not the member. Thus, as shown in Appendix A, we have rules for **.c.a, .c~.a**, and so on. Yet the **.a** suffix *does not* appear in the suffix list since it can never be a **{from suffix}**.

5.7   Special Targets

The **special targets** are a mixed collection of target names that are used to alter how **make** processes a makefile. We have already encountered one of these special targets when we discussed **.SUFFIXES**. In this section we discuss the remainder of these special targets.

If defined in the makefile, the command lines associated with the **.DEFAULT** target are executed whenever **make** cannot find an explicit target, an inference rule, or a file name for a dependency name. The **.DEFAULT** target replaces the normal error-processing routines used when a dependency name cannot be resolved. Although the documentation for UNIX System V states otherwise, the **$@**, **$%**, and **$<** macros *can* be used in writing the command lines for the **.DEFAULT** macro. The actions of **.DEFAULT** can be seen by adding the following lines to a makefile.

```
.DEFAULT :
        @echo from suffix $<
        @echo target name $@
        @echo member name $%
```

When **make** halts execution because of a command line error or when **make** is interrupted, the target being created is automatically deleted. Even if the target has not yet been modified, it is removed. This is done to protect the integrity of the target, but it is not always desirable. For instance, in the following make rule, the target is a time stamp that should not be removed.

```
.PRECIOUS : psrc

psrc : ${SRC}
        ${PR} $? | ${LP}
        touch $@
```

The **.IGNORE** target also modifies error handling. This target is equivalent to the **-i** option of the **make** command, which was discussed in Chapter 4. Likewise, the **.SILENT** target is equivalent to the **-s** option of the **make** command.

> **Note:** The special targets are targets and must include the ":", which identifies the line as a dependency line.

5.8   Summary

In the previous two chapters, we learned how to write a simple makefile and how the **make** command processes a makefile. Based on these building blocks, this chapter has shown how a makefile can be simplified and also become more generic. The additional features of **make** that were described are as follows:

1. *Combining like make rules*: When we have common command lines but different dependencies, we showed how the single colon can be used to eliminate the duplicate command lines. When several make rules have some common command lines, we saw how we could use the double colon to separate the common command lines from the unique ones.

2. *More on macros*: In this chapter, we added a few more macros to the list of internal macros. We also learned how to use the **D** and **F** suffixes to separate the path name from the file name. We also learned how to use macro string substitution to change the suffix of a macro. Finally, we learned how to use default macros for defining UNIX commands and their options.

3. *Inference rules:* A special type of make rule called the inference rule was introduced. The inference rule allows us to define a generic rule for transforming a file with one suffix to a file with another suffix. While it is a powerful feature of **make**, it is also a complex one.

4. *Include files:* Much as the include statement in 'C' or the COPY statement in COBOL is used to incorporate common source code into many programs, the include line can be used to incorporate common statements into a makefile.

5. *Archive libraries:* Archive libraries present a very special problem in writing a makefile. With an archive library, we are concerned about the member and not the library. In this chapter, we discussed the special features of **make** needed to work with archive libraries. In Chapter 11, we will discuss archive libraries in more detail.

6. *Special targets:* Except for the **.DEFAULT** target, these targets use the dependency line syntax for communicating special information to **make**.

Now that we have discussed all the features of **make**, it is time to use these feature in the actual writing of makefiles. This is the subject of Chapter 6.

CHAPTER 6

Building a Software Package with "make"

6.1   Introduction

In the last three chapters, we learned how to use the **make** command. Now we will apply this knowledge to the building of the software package described in Chapter 1. The material presented in this chapter provides you with the information necessary to write most of the makefiles that you will encounter.

Before discussing the writing of makefiles, we will review the objectives that we wish to achieve. Then, ignoring the contents of the makefiles, we first discuss the makefile structure required to build a software package. Next, we look at how to use include files in the writing of makefiles. After we understand the makefile structure, we delve into their contents by discussing the standard targets and their functions. Finally, because of its importance, we cover the subject of ownership and permissions in greater detail.

6.2   Objectives

Writing makefiles is not unlike writing any other piece of source code: *we must know what we want the software to do before we can write it.* So, before discussing the actual makefiles, we need to know what we are trying to achieve. In Chapter 1, we presented the functional requirements for an automated build system. Restating these requirements in terms of makefiles, we have the following:

1. *Statement of steps to build a software package:* In Chapter 1, we saw how to divide a software package into package objects that come together to make the final package. Furthermore, we saw that package objects are a subset of the total number of components needed to build a software package. We can implement this idea by creating **component makefiles** to build components. In addition, we

77

will build the software package through a **product makefile**. Details about the structure and content of these files and how they control the building of the software package are discussed.

2. *Statement of steps to install a software package*: Once a software package has been built and tested, it needs to be installed into the proper directories with the correct permissions. How this is done in a single-machine environment is shown. In addition, a special section on the subject of ownership and permissions has been included (Section 6.5). In Chapter 8, we discuss this subject in more detail.

3. *Linkage of source change to package object change*: As we have seen in the past few chapters, **make** can test to see if the source is newer than the target. That is all well and good when the source file and target are always present. What happens when the work files are removed after completing a change cycle? Do we start from scratch with the next generation? Or do we bring the pieces of the work source tree back together and proceed as if the work source tree had always existed? How to achieve the latter is shown.

6.3   Hierarchical Structure of makefiles

While it is possible to write one makefile to build the entire package, it is not always very practical. Just as we break down software into discrete functional modules, we break makefiles into functional modules. In fact, as you read this chapter, you will notice that the techniques used for good software development also apply to makefiles.

The basic rule is that there is a makefile for the software package and for each component (or subcomponent). From this we can see that each makefile is only concerned with the building of that portion of the software package that lies within its domain. For a component with no subcomponents, there is a component makefile whose purpose is to build the component. For the software package, there is a product makefile that builds all the components. When a component has subcomponents, the resulting makefile is a blend of the component and product makefiles. This blend occurs because it must build the subcomponents (a product makefile function) and then integrate them into a larger component (a component makefile function). This can be illustrated by adding the makefiles and include files discussed next to the source tree shown in Chapter 1. The result is the source tree shown in Figure 6.1.

6.3.1 Product Makefile

The product makefile performs several important functions, which are as follows:

- It defines the environment for the building of the package,

- It decides which component makefiles need to be executed for each target,

- It performs any software-package-level build functions.

The product makefile shown in Figure 6.2 does all these tasks. Using this figure as a basis for discussion, let's see how each of these requirements is fulfilled.

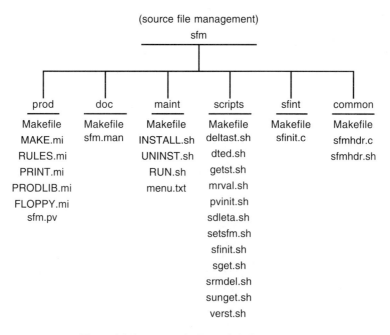

Figure 6.1 Source Tree for Example Software Package

In Section 4.6.1, we discussed the order of precedence in the processing of macro definitions. To summarize, we know that the default order is for macro definitions within a makefile to have precedence over environmental variables, with the command line macro definition providing an override mechanism. This allows us to practice a bit of defensive programming by having the product makefile control the environment.

The definition of the build environment is tackled in three ways:

1. The macro definitions that are common to all makefiles are defined in the include files **MAKE.mi** and **RULES.mi** (see Section 6.3.3 for more details).

2. Any information that is not part of MAKE.mi or RULES.mi is passed to the component makefiles as environmental variables. For example, in Figure 6.2, the variables WDIR and PSID are defined. The last line of .sfmdata file[1] defines PSID, which the **tail** command extracts.

---

[1]The PSID (product SCCS identification number) defines which version of the product version file was used to build the software package. The .sfmdata file is part of this approach to source file management. For additional details, see Israel Silverberry, *Source File Management with SCCS* (Englewood Cliffs, N.J.: Prentice Hall, 1992), Appendix F. For those readers using a different approach to source file management, all references to PSID can be removed.

3. Once the environment has been set, all subsequent executions of **make** use the **-e** option. This approach allows the product makefile to control the actions of the component makefiles by allowing environmental variables to override the default definitions.

Just as the product makefile establishes the environment, it also defines what components are built and the order for building components. The easy way to write such a make rule is as follows:

```
CMPNTS=common sfint scripts

build: ${CMPNTS}

common:
        (WDIR =`dirname \`pwd\``; export WDIR; \
           eval `tail -1 ${WDIR}/.sfmdata`; \
           cd    ${WDIR}/common; \
           ${MAKE} -e -f Makefile ${SGET} build)

sfint:
        (WDIR =`dirname \`pwd\``; export WDIR \
           eval `tail -1 ${WDIR}/.sfmdata`; \
           cd ${WDIR}/sfint; \
           ${MAKE} -e -f Makefile  ${SGET} build)

scripts:
        (WDIR =`dirname \`pwd\``; export WDIR;\
           eval `tail -1 ${WDIR}/.sfmdata`;\
           cd ${WDIR}/scripts; \
           ${MAKE} -e -f Makefile ${SGET} build)
```

This is probably the most common way of writing such a make rule. However, this approach presents several problems. The most noticeable is the repetition of the same commands in each make rule. This repetition will also occur in the targets for install, lint, print clean, and rmbin. Figure 6.2 shows another way to write these make rules. With this approach, the make rules define a list of possible actions, while the CMPNTS and PKG-OBJS macros define the components affected by the action. The CMPNTS and PKGOBJS macros also define the order in which the action affects the components.

Some functions affect all components and are outside the domain of any component. For instance, the definition of the package image tree (image) and the copying of that tree to a package library or to a floppy disk are software package functions. The load and save

targets show how to change the action taken by appending different subsidiary makefiles
to the main makefile.

```
#   Product Makefile for Source File Management Tools
#   %W% %F% %Y% %D% %Q%
#

# Provide relative PATH definition for WDIR, see MAKE.mi
WDIR=..

include RULES.mi
include MAKE.mi

CMPNTS=common sfint scripts
PKGOBJS=sfint scripts
ETREE=${IMAGE} ${IMGDIR} ${IMGDIR}/${SFMDIR}
MFLAGS=-e
LDSAV=PRODLIB.mi

help:
        @echo "Following is a list of valid targets:"
        @echo "  build   - build package in image directory"
        @echo "  install - install on local machine"
        @echo "  print   - print source files"
        @echo "  lint    - check C source files with lint"
        @echo "  clean   - remove work files"
        @echo "  rmbin   - remove objects from image directory"
        @echo "  load    - load image directory with last version"
        @echo "             LDSAV defines the include to be used"
        @echo "              for load and save (default PRODLIB.MI)."
        @echo "  save    - make copy of image directory"
        @echo "build, clean, lint, print, and rmbin can be made for"
        @echo "   ${CMPNTS}"
        @echo "The install target can be made for:"
        @echo "   ${PKGOBJS}"
        @echo "For example, to build the component sfint use"
        @echo "  make build CMPNTS=sfint"

build load:: image

build lint print clean rmbin::
        for i in ${CMPNTS}; do \
                (WDIR =`dirname \`pwd\``; export WDIR; \
                eval `tail -1 ${WDIR}/.sfmdata`; \
                umask ${UMODE}; cd $$WDIR/$$i; ${MAKE} ${MFLAGS} $@); \
        done
```

Figure 6.2 Example of a Product Makefile

```
install: build
        for i in ${PKGOBJS}; do \
                (WDIR =`dirname \`pwd\``; export WDIR; \
                eval `tail -1 ${WDIR}/.sfmdata`; \
                umask ${UMODE}; cd $$WDIR/$$i; ${MAKE} ${MFLAGS} $@); \
        done

load save::
        WDIR =`dirname \`pwd\``; export WDIR; \
                ${MAKE} ${MFLAGS} -f Makefile -f ${LDSAV} x$@

.DEFAULT:
        ${MAKE} ${MFLAGS} help

image: ${ETREE}

${ETREE}:
        mkdir ${MKDFLG} $@
```

Figure 6.2 Example of a Product Makefile (Continued)

6.3.2 Component makefile

Just as the product makefile transfers a directive (build, install, and the like) from the package level to the component level, the component makefile transfers a directive from the component level to actions taken on particular source files. While the total structure remains the same, the details of the component makefile vary according to the objects built by it. Figures 6.3 through 6.5 show the three component makefiles required to build the software package described in Chapter 1. The differences are covered in more detail in the discussions of specific targets.

> **Note:** To independently execute the component makefiles, the path names for all include files must be relative path names. By using relative path names, the work source tree becomes independent of the directory to which it is attached.

```
#   Component Makefile for Source File Management Tools
#
#   Component: sfint
#
#   %W% %F% %Y% %D% %Q%
#
```

Figure 6.3 Component Makefile for "sfint"

```
# Default relative path for WDIR
WDIR=..

include ../prod/RULES.mi
include ../prod/MAKE.mi

CNAME=sfint
IDIR=${IMGDIR}/${SFMDIR}
PDIR=${INSDIR}/${SFMDIR}
FILES=${IDIR}/sfintxx
INSTF=${PDIR}/sfintxx
SRC=sfintxx.c
LINTF=${SRC:.c=.ln}

build install lint print clean rmbin::
        @echo "Starting to $@ ${CNAME}

build:: ${FILES}

install:: ${INSTF}

lint:: ${LINTF}
        ${LINT} ${LTFLAGS} ${LINTF}

print:: prtdate
clean::
        -rm -f *.o *.ln prtdate
rmbin::
        -rm -f ${FILES}
build install lint print clean rmbin::
        @echo "Finished $@ of ${CNAME}

.DEFAULT:
        @echo "No $@ procedure for the ${CNAME} component"

${IDIR}/sfintxx: $$(@F).c ${COMM}/sfmhdr.c
        ${VC} prodver=${RELNUM} reldate=`date '+%D'` \
            cname=${CNAME} machine=${MACHINE} \
        < ${COMM}/sfmhdr.c > idhdr.c
        ${CC} ${CFLAGS} idhdr.c ${@F}.c -o $@
        chmod 600 $@
        -rm idhdr* ${@F}.o

${INSTF}: ${IDIR}/$$(@F)
        ${INSTALL} -f ${@D} -m 600 -u ${OWNER} -g ${GROUP} \
            ${IDIR}/${@F}

include ../prod/PRINT.mi
```

Figure 6.3 Component Makefile for "sfint" (Continued)

```
#   Component Makefile for Source File Management Tools
#   Component: scripts
#   %W% %F% %Y% %D% %Q%
#

# Default relative path for WDIR
WDIR=..

include ../prod/RULES.mi
include ../prod/MAKE.mi

CNAME=scripts
IDIR=${IMGDIR}/${SFMDIR}
PDIR=${INSDIR}/${SFMDIR}
FILES=${IDIR}/deltast ${IDIR}/dted ${IDIR}/getst ${IDIR}/mrval \
    ${IDIR}/pvinit ${IDIR}/sdelta ${IDIR}/setsfm ${IDIR}/sfinit \
     ${IDIR}/sget ${IDIR}/srmdel ${IDIR}/sunget ${IDIR}/verst
INSTF=${PDIR}/deltast ${PDIR}/dted ${PDIR}/getst \
      ${PDIR}/mrval ${PDIR}/pvinit ${PDIR}/sdelta \
      ${PDIR}/setsfm ${PDIR}/sfinit ${PDIR}/sget \
      ${PDIR}/srmdel ${PDIR}/sunget ${PDIR}/verst
SRC=deltast.sh dted.sh getst.sh mrval.sh pvinit.sh sdelta.sh \
      setsfm.sh sfinit.sh sget.sh srmdel.sh sunget.sh verst.sh

build install print clean rmbin::
        @echo "Starting to $@ ${CNAME}

build:: ${FILES}

install:: ${INSTF}

print:: prtdate

clean::
        -rm -f idhdr.sh prtdate

rmbin::
        -rm -f ${FILES}

build install print clean rmbin::
        @echo "Finished $@ of ${CNAME}

.DEFAULT:
        @echo "No $@ procedure for the ${CNAME} component"
```

Figure 6.4 Component Makefile for "scripts"

```
${FILES}: $$(@F).sh ${COMM}/sfmhdr.sh
        ${VC} prodver=${RELNUM} reldate=`date '+%D'` \
            cname=${CNAME} machine=${MACHINE} \
            < ${COMM}/sfmhdr.sh > idhdr.sh
        ${CAT} idhdr.sh ${@F}.sh > $@
        chmod +x $@
        rm idhdr.sh

${INSTF}: ${IDIR}/$$(@F)
        ${INSTALL} -f ${@D} -m 755 -u ${OWNER} -g ${GROUP} \
            ${IDIR}/${@F}

include ../prod/PRINT.mi
```

Figure 6.4 Component Makefile for "scripts" (Continued)

```
  Component Makefile for Source File Management Tools
#
#  Component: common
#
#   %W% %F% %Y% %D% %Q%
#

# Default relative path for WDIR
WDIR=..

include ../prod/RULES.mi
include ../prod/MAKE.mi

CNAME=common
MFLAGS=print
SRC=sfmhdr.c sfmhdr.sh

print clean::
@echo "Starting to $@ ${CNAME}

print:: prtdate
```

Figure 6.5 Component Makefile for "common"

```
clean::
        -rm -f prtdate

print clean::
        @echo "Finished $@ of ${CNAME}

.DEFAULT:
        @echo "No $@ procedure for the ${CNAME} component"

include ../prod/PRINT.mi
```

Figure 6.5 Component Makefile for "common" (Continued)

6.3.3 Standardization through Include Files

The include file, a file specified as part of an include line (see Section 5.5), serves many purposes within a makefile. It plays an important role by providing a standard set of macro definitions to each makefile. Without the include file, these definitions would have to be defined in every makefile or would have to be passed as environmental variables. Macro definitions repeated in every makefile are prone to errors and increase the amount of effort required to make changes. On the other hand, passing all macros as environmental variables from the product makefile makes execution of the component makefile without using the product makefile very difficult.

It is easy to forget that makefiles are source files and that the same techniques used in writing efficient programs can be used for writing efficient makefiles. For example, some make rules, whether explicit or inference rules, could be written so that they become usable in more than one makefile. By using include files for global make rules and global macro definitions, the amount of time required to both write and test a makefile is reduced.

Building a software package for different environments may require a different set of macro definitions. By placing the include file name in a macro definition (see Section 5.5), the macro definition can be changed via a command line macro definition. Or, as a variation on this theme, it can be done by concatenating different description files onto a makefile (see Section 4.5.2). One way to use this idea is shown in Figure 6.2. Other possibilities for this technique include the building of the same software package for different machines or different customers, and so forth.

In the following sections, we look at the various include files referenced by the above makefiles. The reasons for the include file are also discussed. Along the way, a few hints on how to write your own makefile are provided.

"MAKE.mi" Include File

As shown in Figure 6.6, this makefile contains the macro definitions that are related to the software package. Normally, include files, once written and debugged, rarely change. However, the **"MAKE.mi"** include file must change with every release of the software package, since it contains the definition of the release number (RELNUM). From Figures 6.3 and 6.4, we see that the release number is part of the package object identification information.

```
#  Make Variables Used to Build Source Management Tools
#
#  %W% %F% %Y% %D% %Q%

# Shell Macro Definitions
SHELL=/bin/sh
PATH=/bin:/usr/bin:/etc:/usr/sfm:
UMODE=022

# Package Macro Definitions
GROUP=local
MACHINE=i386
OWNER=local
RELNUM=1.1

# Root Directory Macro Definitions
COMM=${WDIR}/common
IMAGE=${WDIR}/image
IMGDIR=${IMAGE}/usr
INSDIR=/usr
SFMDIR=sfm
```

Figure 6.6 "MAKE.mi" Include File

"RULES.mi" Include File

While the **MAKE.mi** include file is oriented to a specific software package, the **RULES.mi** (see Figure 6.7) defines the macros and inference rules related to the *build environment*. The most obvious expression of this is the list of macro definitions that defines each tool used in any makefile. This list of macro definitions is supplemented with new inference rules. The first inference rule defines the transformation of a 'C' source file into a lint file. The remaining inference rules disable the default inference rules related to SCCS.

Should every UNIX utility used be defined as a macro? After all, how much effect does the **rm** command or the **pr** command have on the shape of the final package? Actually, defining every command as a variable offers several advantages:

1. It provides a means of substituting commands without modifying the makefile. For instance, the **cat** command could be used in place of the **pr** command by using the following command line:

```
$ make print PR=cat
```

2. When the development group and the configuration management group use different machines, the control of every utility used helps ensure that the build can be successfully reproduced. When building UNIX and testing UNIX utilities, it may be necessary to define explicit path names for every command.

On the other hand, providing a macro definition for every utility does have disadvantages, such as the following:

1. Extensive use of macros reduces the readability of the file. For example, if the macro definition for PR was the **cat** command, then someone might misread the makefile. Just as macros add flexibility, they also hide information.

2. As the number of utilities used in building a software package increases, the RULES.mi include file becomes more unwieldy.

3. Since the PATH variable is set in MAKE.mi, the search path for utilities is already limited.

In this work, the middle ground is followed by providing macro definitions for all utilities that actively change a package object. Unless the default description file is not used (**make -r**), it defines the minimum number of macro definitions for utilities.

The deletion of the SCCS-related inference rules deserves additional comment. As stated in Chapter 5, the SCCS inference rules assume that the SCCS source tree and work source tree are one in the same. For the reasons pointed out in Chapter 1, this is not a viable practice. Thus, these inference rules are useless vestiges and should be disabled to prevent any confusion. Furthermore, there should not be a link between the building of a software package and SCCS. This separation needs to be maintained for the following reasons:

1. We are building a package for which the SID of each SCCS file is listed in the product version file. Therefore, we are not concerned about the relationship of the date stamp on the SCCS file to that of the source file.

2. As we shall see when we discuss the build target, the critical relationship is between the delta time of the source file, as defined in the delta table section of the SCCS file, and the resulting output module, as defined in the image directory. The testing of this relationship in the dependency line is beyond the capabilities of **make**.

"PRINT.mi" Include File

Figure 6.8 shows another use for an include file. Every component makefile shown previously has a print target. Since this explicit make rule is common to all the component makefiles, it should be written as an include file. Using this technique simplifies both the writing of makefiles and the modification of the make rule.

```
#  Make Rules Used to Build Source Management Tools
#
#  %W% %F% %Y% %D% %Q%

INSTALL=install
LINT=lint
LTFLAGS=
LPFLAGS=
MKDFLG=-p -m 775
PR=pr
PRFLAGS=
SFLAGS=
VC=vc

.SUFFIXES: .ln

.c.ln:
        ${LINT} ${LTFLAGS} -c $<

# disable default rules related to SCCS
.sh~.sh:;

.c~.o:;

.c~.c:;

.sh~:;

.c~:;
```

Figure 6.7 "RULES.mi" Include File

```
#   Print Make Rule Used to Build Source Management Tools
#
#   %W% %F% %Y% %D% %Q%
#
#   Requires that the following macros be defined in the Makefile
#       SRC=list of source files
#
.PRECIOUS: prtdate

prtdate: ${SRC}
        ${PR} ${PRFLAGS} $? | lp ${LPFLAGS}
        touch $@
```

Figure 6.8 "PRINT.mi" Include File

Why not include the above make rule as part of RULES.mi? There are several reasons for this choice:

1. The first explicit make rule defined in RULES.mi would become the default rule for the makefile. As a result, explicit make rules such as "help" would no longer be the default. Moving the include line is not a solution since it alters the precedence of macro definitions.

2. As explained in Section 5.5, *macros used in include files, but not defined in the include file, must be defined before the include file.* Thus, the macro ${SRC} must be defined before PRINT.mi.

At this point, it should be apparent that it is possible to create a set of standard include files that can be used in the makefiles for many software packages.

"PRODLIB.mi" and "FLOPPY.mi" Include Files

While the purpose of the make rules defined in these include files (see Figures 6.9 and 6.10) is discussed in the next section, they do show another technique that can be used in the writing of makefiles. In Section 4.5.2, we discussed how two or more makefiles could be concatenated into one makefile. Using this technique, plus using the macro ${LDSAV} to define the name of the file to be concatenated, we can create a different makefile when the makefile is reprocessed.

This technique is useful in the following conditions:

1. The use of concatenation allows portions of a makefile to be included optionally. Thus, as shown in Figure 6.2, PRODLIB.mi is only included when we wish to reference the make rules it contains.

2. By defining the name as a macro, we can change the file that is to be concatenated by simply giving a new macro definition on the command line. For example, the command line:

$ make save LDSAV=FLOPPY.mi

will change the rules for saving the image directory.

```
#   prodlib make rule
#
#   %W% %F% %Y% %D% %Q%
#
CPIO=cpio

PRDLIB=/prodlib

xload:
        cd ${PRDLIB}/${PROD}/${RELNUM}; \
                find . -depth -print | \
                ${CPIO} -pdmv ${IMAGE}

xsave: ${PRDLIB}/${PROD} ${PRDLIB}/${PROD}/${RELNUM}
        cd ${IMAGE}; find . -depth -print | \
                ${CPIO} -pdmv ${PRDLIB}/${PROD}/${RELNUM}

${PRDLIB}/${PROD} ${PRDLIB}/${PROD}/${RELNUM}:
        mkdir -m 770 $@
        chgrp ${GROUP} $@
        chown ${OWNER} $@
```

Figure 6.9 "PRODLIB.mi" Include File

```
#   floppy make rule
#
#   %W% %F% %Y% %D% %Q%
#
CPIO=cpio
FORMAT=format
FMTFLG=
LABELIT=labelit
MKFS=mkfs
MOUNT=mount
UMOUNT=umount

FLPBLK=2048
FLPCYL=32
FLPDEV=/dev/dsk/f0q15dt
FLPGAP=2
FLPIND=256
FLPLBL=${PROD}${RELNUM}
FLPRDEV=/dev/rdsk/f0q15dt
MNTDIR=mnt

xload xsave::
        @echo 'Insert Floppy Disk in Drive 0, then type <ENTER>'
        @line > /dev/null 2>&1

xload::
        ${MOUNT} ${FLPDEV} /${MNTDIR}
        cd /${MNTDIR}; find . -depth -print | \
            ${CPIO} -pdmv ${IMAGE}

xsave::format
        ${MOUNT} ${FLPDEV} /${MNTDIR}
        cd ${IMAGE}; find . -depth -print | \
            ${CPIO} -pdmv /${MNTDIR}

xload xsave::
        ${UMOUNT} ${FLPDEV}

format:
        @echo 'Formatting Distribution Disk'
        ${FORMAT} ${FMTFLG} ${FLPRDEV}
        ${MKFS} ${FLPRDEV} ${FLPBLK}:${FLPIND} ${FLPGAP} ${FLPCYL}
        ${LABELIT} ${FLPRDEV} ${MNTDIR} ${FLPLBL}
```

Figure 6.10 "FLOPPY.mi" Include File

6.4   Standard Targets

The preceding makefiles contain two types of targets: **action targets** and **object targets**. An action target states the type of action to be taken (for example, build, install, print, or clean) and is the target that the user specifies, whereas an object target is the object action set forth in the action target. The object target may be the name of component makefiles, as shown in the product makefile, or source and work files, as shown in the component makefiles.

The distinction between action targets and object targets is important in that the user does not select object targets. Only action targets are selected by the user. Based on the action target selected by the user, the make rule specifies which object targets are to be made. The action targets discussed next represent a basic list of such targets.

6.4.1 'help' Target

The makefile is truly a black box. There is no automatic menu system from which one can choose the action target to be made. Normally, without a listing of the makefile, we have no idea of what action targets are available. To overcome this limitation, it is recommended that the first explicit make rule be 'help'.

As shown in Figure 6.2, the 'help' target provides a list of valid action targets and the rules for altering the list of object targets. Although not shown, the component makefiles (Figures 6.3, 6.4, and 6.5) also could have a 'help' target.

6.4.2 'build' Target

The 'build' target has one primary object, the building of the components of the software package and placing the results in the image directory. For this action target, all the work takes place in the component makefiles.

> **Golden Rule!** The dependencies for components stored in the image directory must be the source files maintained by SCCS and not intermediate work files.

To understand this rule, we need to consider the development cycle and how it is related to the build process. Using Figure 6.3 as a point of discussion, let's say that the building of **sfintxx** was as follows:

```
${IDIR}/sfintxx: $$(@F).c idhdr.o
  ${CC} ${CFLAGS} idhdr.o ${@F}.c -o $@ ${LFLAGS}
  chmod u+s
  -rm ${@F}.o
```

```
idhdr.o: ${COMM}/sfmhdr.c
        ${VC} prodver=${RELNUM reldate=`date '+%D'` \
                cname=${CNAME} machine=${MACHINE} \
                < ${COMM}/sfmhdr.c > ${@:.o=.c}
        ${CC} ${CFLAGS} -c ${@:.o=.c
        -rm -f :.c}
```

The dependency line for **sfintxx** seems like a perfectly logical way to define the relationship. So what is wrong with it? If idhdr.o does not exist, it is made, although sfmhdr.c has not changed. Since idhdr.o is newer than **sfintxx**, it is made although there were no source file changes. This problem can be demonstrated by executing **make clean**, which removes all intermediate work files, followed by **make build**.

In terms of the development cycle, the preceding means that **sfintxx** is always made although no source files have been changed between versions. From the point of view of quality assurance, it means that **sfintxx** has to be tested since it has been recompiled. However, if we use the method shown in Figure 6.3, then **sfintxx** will only be compiled if either sfintxx.c or sfmhdr.c changes.

There is one fly in the ointment. When a file is retrieved from SCCS with the **get** command, whether to initially build the work source tree or to get back an accidentally deleted file, the date stamp on the file will be the current date and time. To the **make** command, this will be treated as if the file had changed. The correct date and time for the file should be the delta date and time for the SID retrieved.[2] To correct this problem, the **touch** command can be used to correct the date and time stamps.

_____

[2]In Silverberg, *Source File Management with SCCS*, special interfaces to the **get** command were described. By adding the following lines to the **getst** and **sget** commands, the correct date and stamp can be created:

1.The **getst** command

```
at line:
166get -r$FSID -s $SDIR/$CDIR/$SFILE
add the following lines:
  GFILE=`echo $SFILE | sed 's/..//'`
  DTIME=`prs -r$FSID -d":Dm::Dd::Th::Tm::Dy:" \
   $SDIR/$CDIR/$SFILE`
  touch $DTIME $GFILE
```

2.The **sget** command

```
at line:
151GETOK=0
add the following lines:
  GFILE=`echo $SNAME | sed 's/..//'`
  DTIME=`prs $RSID -d":Dm::Dd::Th::Tm::Dy:" $SPATH`
  touch $DTIME $GFILE
```

These instructions are based on the principle that, for the build of a component to be valid, it must have the SCCS identification keyword strings expanded. So, if a file was changed, it would have to be delta'ed, retrieved, and built again to have the correct strings. Thus, the delta date should always be older than the matching component date.

6.4.3 'install' Target

Once we have completed testing of a software package, it is ready to be installed into the local "production" environment. The objective of the 'install' target is to move the software package to the production directory on the local machine (the target machine). The approach covered in this section reflects a traditional view regarding installation of software packages. In Chapter 8, an alternative approach to installation is discussed that does not depend on the development machine and target machine being one machine.

The component makefiles handle the installing of package objects. By transferring the task to the component makefiles, the product makefile needs to know which components build package objects. If the image directory is not re-created every time a new version of a software package is built (see the preceding discussion), then only those package objects that have changed will be installed. This is as it should be. Besides copy package objects, installation involves issues of ownership of and permissions for the various package objects in the software package. These topics are sufficiently complicated for a separate section to be devoted to them (Section 6.5).

As to the mechanics of installation, Figures 6.3 and 6.4 use the **install** command. Using Figure 6.3 as an example, the 'install' make rule could just have easily been written as

```
cp ${IDIR}/${@F} $@
chm10 $@
chgrROUP} $@
chown ${OWNER} $@
```

As we shall see in Section 6.5, whether using the **install** command or separate commands, the 'install' target may require super-user permission.

6.4.4 'clean' and 'rmbin' Targets

Each component makefile has a 'clean' target, which removes any extraneous work files created by the component makefile. After the 'clean' target has been executed, the source tree for each component should be the same as when it was retrieved from SCCS. For a new software package, it should only contain those source files that are to be stored in the source library. *It does not remove any files from the image directory.*

> **Note:** If a makefile has been written correctly, you should be able to do a **make clean** followed by a **make build** and not cause any targets to be remade because a work file was removed.

The 'rmbin' target is the "make clean" for the image directory. It removes any objects created by the component makefile that were placed in the image directory.

6.4.5 'print' and 'lint' Targets

These action targets are administrative targets because they are not required for the building of the package. The category of administrative targets includes any target that is not critical to the building of a package object. By their very nature, administrative targets must be passive targets with respect to the source files and the package objects.

Note: Action targets that serve as administrative targets must not alter a file in such a way as to affect any other target. In other words, they must not modify the time stamp, which in turn would cause the 'build' target to think that the source file has changed.

Besides being an administrative target, the 'print' target shows how to implement a temporary date stamp file. Notice that the file "prtdate" is removed by clean, just as any other work file would be removed. The 'lint' target provides an example of how to write a new inference rule.

6.4.6 'load' and 'save' Targets

Throughout this chapter, there has been a constant emphasis on the importance of building only that which has changed. These targets serve to preserve the image directory from one version of the software package to the next. Thus, by combining the original image file with source files that have the delta time as the time stamp for the file, we preserve the build environment from one generation of software to the next. The result is a reduction in the test effort required to check the validity of the software package.

The names of the targets describe the function of each target. From our discussion of FLOPPY.mi and PRODLIB.mi, we saw that there are at least two ways of implementing the objective. Whether the image directory is stored on a floppy disk or a tape or in a directory is not important. What is important is that the image directory is stored and re-stored in a way that does not alter the time stamps on any of the files.

6.4.7 '.DEFAULT' Target

Although there are many other possible uses for the '.DEFAULT' target, two possible uses were shown in the preceding makefiles. In the product makefile, the '.DEFAULT' target forces the execution of the 'help' target by re-executing the makefile with the new target. In the component makefile, the target merely issues a message that the target is not implemented. By using it as an informational message, it is possible to write a product makefile that is generic and yet provide a positive response to exceptions within the component makefile.

6.5   A Word on Ownership and Permissions

This section is not a tutorial on how UNIX handles file security.[3] Rather, the intent is to discuss the questions of ownership and permissions that must be faced when installing a software package. What should be the owner ID and group ID of the installed package objects? In addition, what permissions should be assigned to these package objects? It is hoped that the following sections will shed some light on these questions.

The following sections are based on maintaining a secure environment. In practice, this means that a user can only alter the files and directories that are part of his or her *home* directory. The system administrator is the only person allowed to alter files and directories that are not part of any *login account*, which means that only the system administrator is allowed to install a software package into a production directory.

6.5.1 Suggestions about Ownership

Unless there is a good reason to do otherwise, no software package should be installed in one of the standard directories (for example, /bin, /etc, and even /usr/bin). Software vendors should create their own set of directories. Software developed in-house should either be installed in directory names that identify the software package or standard local directory equivalents of the standard directories. This strategy helps prevent unidentified files from sneaking into the system. For example, the package objects for the source file management package are installed in a directory called */usr/sfm*.

Just as standard directories should not be used, the standard owner and group IDs (bin, sys, adm) should be avoided whenever possible. Although this seems a bit extreme, minimizing the opportunities for security violation is an important element in maintaining a secure environment. This is especially true when package objects with SUID and SGID permission are installed.

Implementation of this idea requires the creation of one or more *non-login accounts* equivalent to the **bin** account. In some environments, one such account will be sufficient. In other environments, several such accounts may be required to separate the different software packages. For example, we could have an account called local with a directory entry in /etc/passwd as follows:

```
local:NONE:10:50:0000-Local(0000):/usr/local:
```

Just as separate owners should be used, separate groups should be used. Following the preceding example, we could create an entry in /etc/group as follows:

```
local::50:root,bin,daemon
```

---

[3]If you are interested in more information about UNIX file security, the following are two excellent sources of information: X/Open Company, Ltd., *X/Open Security Guide* (Englewood Cliffs, N.J.: Prentice Hall, 1989); and Patrick H. Wood and Stephen G. Kochan, *UNIX System Security* (Hasbrouck Heights, N.J.: Hayden Book Company, Inc., 1985).

This entry parallels the group entry for bin and is sufficient for most installation requirements. However, should we wish to use the group ID for controlling access, separate group accounts are required.

> **Warning!**   Never use the owner ID or group ID of the software package manager as the ID for a production directory or file. To do so means that the software package manager can install the software package into the production directory. As stated, the responsibility for installing a software package falls on the system administrator.

6.5.2 Suggestions about Permissions

From the point of view of the 'install' target, we are only concerned with the permissions of the files to be installed in directories that have already been established by the system administrator. So, before taking a brief look at directory permissions, we shall discuss the problem of file permissions.

The most important permission is that granted to "others." If you question this statement, look at the commands that you execute. Unless you are executing your own commands or are logged into a system account, you are neither the owner of nor a member of the group for the commands that you execute. This leaves only one class of permissions left - "others". Thus, "others" must have execute permission for all executable files and read permission for shell scripts and other files that are processed by an interpreter. *Write permission should never be granted to "others."*

The second most important permission is that granted to the "group." If you do not want everyone to have access to the installed file (as occurs with SUID programs), the next line of defense is the group permissions. The permissions to be assigned to the group follow the same guidelines as permissions for "others."

The least important permission is that granted to the "owner." If we follow the guidelines for owner ID presented in the preceding discussion, then this permission only has value when referenced by the system administrator. *The "owner" is the only user to be allowed write permission for the file.*

Now that we have a better understanding of file permissions, we need to consider permissions for directories. The *X/Open Security Guide*[4] divides directories into one of eight categories depending on whether it is static or dynamic on one dimension and private, pass-through, informational, or public on the other dimension. Unless you have special security requirements, most production directories can be considered as dynamic and informational. This translates to a permission of *drwxr-xr-x* or (755). When access is to be restricted so that the group controls access the permission would be *drwxr-x---* or (750).

---

[4]*X/Open Security Guide*, p. 96.

6.5.3 Danger of SUID or SGID programs

Because they alter the permissions for the user, SUID and SGID programs have to be carefully monitored. This is one case where control of execution through groups becomes very important. To reduce any risk of security violations by overlaying a valid SUID program with a *Trojan horse*, write permission should be granted only to the owner.

6.6   Summary

In this chapter we reviewed the entire system of makefiles required to build the software package that was first described in Chapter 1. The makefiles and include files shown in this chapter can be used as models for other packages. Often, nothing more than the macro definitions have to be changed. However, this is not the end of the story. In the remainder of this work, we will discuss special problems and how they can be solved. In Chapter 12, we will again look at this simple package, but in a different light

CHAPTER 7

Tools Management

7.1   Introduction

> Tools must be managed, just as source files are managed.

Tools management means that we are going to control the version of the software tools used to build a software package. This applies to any executable program (for example, 'C' compiler), object library (libc.a), or source file (the include files) that is not a part of the software package. In other words, we are talking about any file that is external to the software package and that affects the binary image produced. Whether the software tool is "home grown" or received from an outside party is not relevant.

Although you may think that this chapter does not apply to you, stop a minute and read the rest of this section and then decide. First, ask yourself if binary reproducibility is important. For example, in a typical software development organization, the development group builds a software package and then turns the final package plus the source over to a configuration management group. They, in turn, build the software package, again based on the source and instructions received from the development group, and see if the results are the same. Of course, if each group used different versions of the same software tools to build a package, the result may be different. This could influence the results of any tests.

If the preceding scenario does not apply to you, consider this situation. The same software package is being distributed to several customers. However, for whatever reason, not every customer has the same environment. As a result, different versions of the tools have to be used for different customers.

If neither condition applies, this chapter may not apply to your build environment. If it does apply, continue reading.

The first item we need to discuss is the idea of a **tools library**. We then show how to modify the makefiles shown in Chapter 6 so that they use the tools library. Next, we look at the problems in creating software tools that work correctly in this environment. Finally, we learn how to install a software tool into the tools library.

7.2   Tools Library

Just as we have a source library (/srclib) for source files and a product library (/prodlib) for the storage of software images, we need a tools library to track the different versions of tools. This library could be structured as shown in Figure 7.1.

Based on the breakdown of UNIX utilities shown in the *Unix System V: Programmer's Guide,*[1] the System V tools used in building software have been divided between the 'C' Compiler System (ccs) and the Software Generation Utilities (sgu). The third tools package is for the Source File Management (sfm) utilities mentioned in Chapter 1. We will call these divisions **software tool packages**. Under each software tool package, a directory is created for each version of the tool, and then additional directories follow the version directory for the various components.

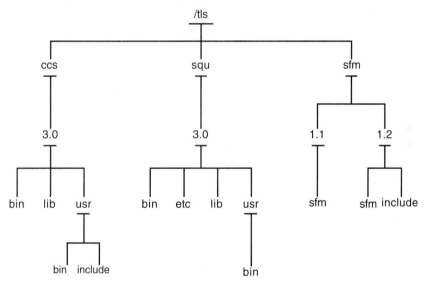

Figure 7.1 Structure of Tools Library

Breaking up the UNIX utilities into separate directories is not absolutely necessary when they are part of the total UNIX release. However, when the software tool packages

---

[1]AT&T, *UNIX System V: Programmer's Guide* (Englewood Cliffs, N.J.: Prentice Hall, 1987), Appendix A.

are purchased as separate software packages, it is important to keep the packages in separate directories.

By using the tools library, it is possible to specify exactly what tools are to be used in building a software package. In the next section, we see how to define the version of the tools used by **make**.

7.3   A Tools-independent Build

In Chapter 6, we defined a file called **RULES.mi**, which contained macro definitions for every software tool used in the makefiles. By modifying only this file, we can make the entire build process independent of the location of the tools. Let's look at Figure 7.2 and see what has been changed from the version shown in Figure 6.7.

First, three macros definitions were added to define the locations of the tools to be used (**TLSCCS**, **TLSSFM**, and **TLSSGU**). By merely changing these macro definitions, a different version of each tool could be used. Each tool that affects the binary image of the package object has been modified to use the appropriate macro definition.

Although this forces the correct tool to be executed, it is not all that has to be changed. Some tools, such as **as** or **cc**, have internal references that must also be controlled. After all, it would accomplish very little if the tools, libraries, and include files referenced by these executables belonged to a different version than the one stated. To specify the location of these files, we must use the **-Y** flag for **AS**, **CC** (older versions of the 'C' Compiler may use the **-B** and the **-t** flags in place of the **-Y** flag), and **LD** (see the appropriate manual page[2] for more details).

For those utilities that are not in need of version control, the exact path name has been given to ensure that the released version of the utility is used. Again, this is a defensive practice to ensure that everything is controlled, which, in turn, should help guarantee that the build is reproducible.

In theory, we should now have formulated a build process in which all the elements are controlled. However, this is a myth. Although is not used in this example, yacc has a reference to /usr/lib/yaccpar whose location cannot be altered. This brings us to the next topic: how to develop software tools that are not dependent on being in a certain directory.

```
#Make Rules Used to Build Source Management Tools
#
#   %W% %F% %Y% %D% %Q%
# definition of special tools directories
```

Figure 7.2 RULES.mi for Tools Independence

[2]AT&T, U*NIX System V: Programmer's Reference Manual* (Englewood Cliffs, N.J.: Prentice Hall, 1987), pp. 10, 12, 25, 57.

```
TLSCCS=/tls/ccs/3.0
TLSSFM=/tls/sfm/1.1
TLSSGU=/tls/sgu/3.0
# definition of tools
AR=${TLSSGU}/bin/ar
AS=${TLSSGU}/bin/as
ASFLAGS=
ASTOOLS=-Y m,${M4}
CC=${TLSCCS}/bin/cc
CFLAGS=-O
CTOOLS=-Y p,${TLSCCS}/lib -Y 0,${TLSCCS}/lib \
       -Y 2,${TLSCCS}/lib -Y a,${TLSSGU}/bin \
       -Y b,${TLSCCS}/lib -Y 1,${TLSSGU}/bin \
       -Y S,${TLSCCS}/lib -Y I,${TLSCCS}/usr/include \
       -Y L,${TLSCCS}/lib -Y U,${TLSSGU}/lib
GET=${TLSSFM}/sfm/sget
INSTALL=${TLSSGU}/etc/install
LD=${TLSSGU}/bin/ld
LDFLAGS=
LDTOOLS= -Y L,${TLSCCS}/lib -Y U,${TLSSGU}/lib
LEX=${TLSSGU}/usr/bin/lex
LINT=/usr/bin/lint
LTFLAGS=
LPFLAGS=
M4=${TLSSGU}/usr/bin/m4
MAKE=${TLSSGU}/bin/make
MKDFLG=-p -m 775
PR=/bin/pr
PRFLAGS=
SFLAGS=
VC=${TLSSGU}/usr/bin/vc

.SUFFIXES: .ln

.c.ln:
       ${LINT} ${LTFLAGS} -c $<

# disable default rules related to SCCS
.sh~.sh:;
.c~.o:;

.c~.c:;

.sh~:;

.c~:;
```

Figure 7.2 RULES.mi for Tools Independence (Continued)

7.4   Tools Independence and Program Design

The design of software tools to allow different versions to exist on one computer is not a standard practice. In fact, the *X/Open Portability Guide,*[3] which is based on UNIX System V Release 2.0, does not refer to the **-Y** flag (or the older **-B** and **-t** flags[4])   When using standard utilities, be alert to the possibility that there may be references to uncontrolled tools, libraries, and other files that may affect the result.

In this section, we will be concerned with the issues involved in the designing of software tools that will work correctly in a *tools-independent* environment. The following sections are ordered by the different types of problems that may be encountered in writing software that is independent of its external environment.

7.4.1 Search Path for Executable Files

Hard-coded search paths for executable programs must be avoided. Providing the complete patname, such as /bin/cc, automatically makes it impossible to make a software tool independent of its environment. How then do we control which program will be executed?

The easiest way is to let the system use the **PATH** environmental variable. Thus, we can control the search path by defining **PATH** to include the correct directories in the **tools library**. While this is the simplest approach, it does have a major drawback, *security of SUID or SGID programs.* To better understand the problem, let's consider the program **sfintxx**, which was built in Chapter 6. In essence, this program is an interface to the SCCS commands. When executed, this program gives the user the same permission as the owner of the program **sfintxx**. The aim of this program is to enhance SCCS security. But what would happen to security if the **PATH** variable were used to control which program was to be executed?

It would not take a great amount of effort for a disgruntled employee to compromise the integrity of the system. He or she would only need to create a program or shell script (a *Trojan horse)* with the name of an SCCS program and then alter the **PATH** variable so that the *Trojan horse* was used instead of the real program. Since **sfintxx** would cause the *Trojan horse* to be executed with the permission of the owner of **sfintxx,** this program could create, modify, or delete files at will!

In **sfintxx**, explicit path names for all SCCS commands are used since SCCS is not a controlled tool for the building of software packages. But what could be done if the program to be executed had to use a controlled software tool? Obviously, using the **PATH** variable is not a valid option. Moreover, any option that allows the path name to be altered presents a possible security risk. *The X/Open Security Guide*[5] recommends a

---

[3]X-Open Company, Ltd., *X/Open Portability Guide, Volume I: XSI Commands and Utilities* (Englewood Cliffs, N.J.: Prentice Hall, 1989), p. 58.

[4]T.A. Dolotta, S.B. Olsson, A.G. Petruccelli, eds., *UNIX User's Manual Release 3.0* (Murray Hill, N.J.: Bell Laboratories,Inc., June 1980), see cc(1).

[5]X/Open Company, Ltd., *X/Open Security Guide* (Englewood Cliffs, N.J.: Prentice Hall, 1989), p. 58.

series of special precautions that should be taken for SUID or SGID programs. These precautions include the following:

1. Always identify the real user via the **getuid()** system call.

2. Have an authorization file for users who are allowed special permission.

3. Log all uses of the SUID or SGI program, including attempts to take illegal actions.

For our purposes, the special log file could contain the full path name of any commands that are executed. This would then allow the use of an option equivalent to the **-Y** option, as described previously. Furthermore, the SUID or SGID program could limit alternative paths to certain path names, such as the production directory or the Tools Library.

For shell scripts that use SUID or SGID programs,[6] we can use a variable to define the default path. This variable could then be altered by either an environmental variable or a command line option. For example, if we were to use environmental variables to control the location of DELTA and GET, we could write the interface to these programs as follows:

```
SFMDIR=${SFMDIR:-'/usr/sfm'}
DELTA='$SFMDIR/sfint$PROD -Cdelta'
GET='$$FMDIR/sfint$PROD -Cget'
```

From this, we can see that it is possible to create software tools that are independent of any particular environment. There is a side benefit to environmental independence. When software is not dependent on a specific environment, testing of the software can be done without altering the released software.

7.4.2 References to External Files

This is actually a much easier problem than the preceding one. The rule is very simple: *all references to external files must have a means of specifying an alternative path.* Thus, default path names are perfectly acceptable, but there must be a way to override the default. This can be done either through environmental variables or through command line options such as the **-Y** option.

The source file management software defined in Chapter 1 has a hard-coded reference to the location of the work files for the Modification Request Numbers. In this case, the flag option is not viable since the program is forked from the **delta** command, which does not provide any means of passing options. Since the environment is passed to **mrval**

---

[6]For those who have implemented the Source File Management Tools defined in Silverberg, *Source File Management with SCCS* (Englewood Cliffs, N.J.: Prentice Hall, 1992) and who want to modify them to be part of the tools library, a few changes have to be made. The scripts for **deltast**, **dted**, **sdelta**, **sget**, **srmdel**, **sunget**, and **verst** need to have the definition of the PATH variable removed and the lines shown in the text need to be added.

from **delta**, we can use an environmental variable. Again, as previously, we will provide a default for the normal execution.

```
VFILE=${MRDIR:-'/usr/mradm'}/valmr
LFILE=${MRDIR:-'/usr/mradm'}/logmr
```

7.5   Installing a Software Package in the Tools Library

Just as we have a special target for the installation of a software package into the production directory, we can create a target that will install a package into the tools library. Since the only change is the name of the directory into which the package is to be installed, we need only to add a new macro definition to **MAKE.mi** and a new target to the product makefile.

1. To **MAKE.mi** add:

```
TLSDIR=/tls/sfm/${RELNUM}
```

2. To the product makefile add:

```
mktool:
        -rm -rf ${TLSDIR}
     WDIR=`dirname \`pwd\``; export WDIR; \
            ${MAKE} ${MFLAGS} image \
            "IMAGE=${TLSDIR}" \
            "IMGDIR=${TLSDIR}"
     WDIR=`dirname \`pwd\``; export WDIR; \
            ${MAKE} ${MFLAGS} install \
            "INSDIR=${TLSDIR}"
```

This shows another reason why it is important to use macro definitions. Without any changes to the component makefiles, we have been able to implement a new action target in the product makefile. All we did was change the definition of **INSDIR** by using a command line macro definition and reexecuting the same makefile. A little sneaky, but it works and it solves the problem.

7.6   Summary

This chapter shows how we can achieve binary reproducibility at different times or on different machines by using a tools library. We looked at how we could modify the **RULES.mi** include file to use the tools library for those software tools that affect the binary image of a package object. For many software packages, this would be the end of the line.

For those who are responsible for developing software tools, we discussed the design criteria for software tools that are to be a part of the tools library. The critical issue is that all external references, whether they are executable or data files, have the option of being changed either by environmental variables or command line options. Finally, we discussed how a new version of a software tool could be installed into the tools library.

CHAPTER 8

Software Package Administration

8.1   Introduction

In today's world of desk-top computers, software vendors are not the only ones faced with the problem of installing a software package on multiple machines. The makefile system described in Chapter 6 assumes that a software package is built and installed on the same machine.[1] In this chapter, we look at an alternative approach to software package maintenance. The approach considers all software packages to be distributable software. Such a software package must be installed from some type of distribution media (for example, floppy disk or tape). Furthermore, we must be able to remove the software package from the system. It even could be argued that for a single machine all software packages should be installed from a distribution media. With this approach, rebuilding the system is a matter of consecutively adding software packages and then loading any user files.

For many software packages, installation is only the first step on the road to a usable software package. Before they can be used, some software packages require the setting of various configuration options. Besides discussing the content of these package objects, we look at how to integrate them with the *Package Management* option of the **sysadm** command.

8.2   Software Package Maintenance

In the past, when we purchased a software package, the vendor provided a set of instructions on how to install the package. Occasionally, we also received instructions on how to

---

[1]There is a possible exception to this statement. If you are part of a local area network that supports a distributed file system (for example, RFS or NFS), it may be possible to perform installs on multiple systems by changing the definition of the **INSDIR** macro to the path name for each machine.

remove an installed package. There were almost as many ways to install a software package as there were versions of UNIX. In time, the suppliers of UNIX began to provide mechanisms for software package maintenance. Again, each supplier offered a different approach.

Along with the problem of binary incompatibility, the lack of software package maintenance standards made impossible the creation of *shrink-wrapped software*. While the problem of binary incompatibility has yet to be solved, great strides have been made in standards for software package maintenance. Beginning with UNIX System V Release 2.0, the **sysadm** command provides a means of installing, listing, removing, and running software packages. Now, UNIX System V Release 4.0 (SVR4) provides an entire subsystem for the packaging of software.

The utilities provided in SVR4 represent the future direction for software package maintenance. These utilities are fully described in the AT&T documentation[2] and, therefore, are not covered in this work. Instead, this chapter shows how to interface to the *Software Management* utilities of the **sysadm** command. With this approach, those readers who are not using SVR4 are provided the information needed to implement software package maintenance.

8.2.1 Software Management Menu

Although we will concentrate on the *Software Management Menu* option of the **sysadm** command, we should also recognize that the tasks that are performed by this menu should be a part of any software package maintenance system. These basic tasks are the ability to install a software package, produce a list of installed packages, and remove a software package from the system. The ability to run a package without installing it is a nice but not a necessary option.

The real question is how to implement these functions, especially considering that the details will vary from package to package. In the **sysadm** command, they are implemented in the following manner:

1. The distribution media used for installation must be a mountable device and it must be mounted to the directory */install*.

2. The file system name for the distribution media must be "install".

3. The mounted file system must contain a top-level directory called "install". This directory will contain shell scripts or programs as defined next:

```
INSTALL {device} {mount directory} {device name
UNINSTALL {device} {mount directory} {device name}
RUN {device} {mount directory} {device name}
```

---

[2]At&T, *UNIX System V Release 4: Programmer's Guide: System Services and Application Packaging Tools* (Englewood Cliffs, N.J.: Prentice Hall, 1990), Chapter 8.

This technique also makes it relatively simple to execute the functions even on systems that do not have the **sysadm** command. In this situation, one would only have to mount the distribution media, execute the desired command, and then unmount the distribution media.

In the following sections, we will look at each option and show how it can be implemented. By the end of this discussion, we will have a series of models that are easily adaptable to any software package.

8.2.2 Installing a Software Package

The installation of a software package can be defined as *the process of transferring the package from the distribution media to the production media and, optionally, the execution of any one-time actions required to prepare the package for use*. As such, it is functionally equivalent to the 'install' action target defined in Section 6.4.3. The **INSTALL** script shown in Appendix E shows how this objective can be achieved.

Notice that the structure of the file system on the distribution media mirrors the root file system. Using this method, installation is merely a matter of using the **cpio** command to copy the distribution file system to the root file system. This is very important when we want to remove the software package and need to know the location of the files. Also, as we shall see later, it is much easier to create the shell scripts to run a software package when we know its location. Just as important, it makes it possible to write the software so that it can be executed from the distribution media.

Also notice that the **INSTALL** script asks for the owner ID and group ID. These prompts are examples of *one-time install option*s. They allow the system administrator to assign the owner ID and the group ID in accordance with the security guidelines set forth in Chapter 6. However, so as to give the distribution media some degree of protection, the distribution owner ID and group ID should be 'bin'.

The setting of the owner ID and group ID should be a standard procedure for every **INSTALL** script.

Depending on the software package, there may be other one-time install options. One must be careful to distinguish between *one-time install options* and the setting of *default* or *configuration option*s. Decisions about one-time install options are made during installation and are not subject to change after the software package has been installed. On the other hand, default and configuration options can be subject to change. For example, to define a communication's port as part of the install process is a mistake. This should be part of the configuration procedure. Rather than mixing package maintenance actions with configuration actions, tell the user to execute the appropriate configuration option.

8.2.3 List of Installed Packages

To be listed as an *installed package*, a file called **"{prod id}.name"** must be in the "/usr/ options" directory. The list option will then display the {prod id} and contents of the file {prod id}.name. The ".name" file should only contain a short menu description line so that the final menu line will fit on a single line.

> **Note:** *The list option serves only an informational function.* The **sysadm** shell scripts for removing and running a package only display the list of packages. They do not use the list for either selection or verification of the distribution media for the indicated function.

8.2.4 Removing a Software Package

All too often, the emphasis is placed on installing a software package and little consideration is given to the ability to remove an installed package. Yet, to install a new version or to remove a software package that is no longer used, we need a procedure by which we can *ensure that the system is restored to the same condition as it was before the installation of the software package*. The **UNINSTALL** script shown in Appendix E is an example of how this can be achieved.

> **DON'T FORGET**: The "{prod id}.name" file must be removed from the /usr/ options directory when a package is removed.

8.2.5 Running a Software Package

Why would you ever want to run a software package from the distribution media? Here are two possible reasons:

1. If a software package is rarely used, it provides one way of conserving space on the regular file system.

2. It becomes a simple method for creating a demonstration disk for a software package.

The nature of the shell script needed to run a software package from the distribution media will vary from package to package. However, there are implications involving software design that go beyond the mere writing of a special shell script. These issues are similar to those discussed regarding the design of software tools. Besides the requirements mentioned in Section 7.4, the software package must be self-contained. At most, only temporary files should be written on the regular file system, and these temporary files must be removed.

> **Note:** Even if the software package cannot be executed from the distribution media, a **RUN** script should be provided. This dummy **RUN** script could display information about the package, as does the script shown in Appendix E.

8.2.6 How to Build a Distribution Disk

Adding the preceding package objects to the makefile system described in Chapter 6 requires another component directory and component makefile. In addition, we need to make a few modifications to the product makefile and **FLOPPY.mi**.

The first step is to create a new component directory, which we call *maint*. This directory will contain the component makefile (see Figure 8.1),[3] the scripts **INSTALL**, **UNINSTALL**, and **RUN** (see Appendix E), and the file **menu.txt** (see Figure 8.2). The source file **menu.txt** is used to build the file **sfm.name** (see the preceding discussion on the file "{prod id}.name").

Except for the building of **${PROD}.name** and the lack of an install target, the makefile is nothing more than a variation of Figure 6.4. The problem in building **${PROD}.name** is that the output file must contain a single line. Yet, to properly track the source file, we need the SCCS ID keywords. Both goals are achieved by processing the file with the **vc** command. The ":msg" lines will be written to standard error, but not to standard output. Thus, the output file will only contain the one required line. The install target is omitted because the package objects in this component are never installed.

```
#   Component Makefile for Source File Management Tools
#
#   Component: maint
#
#   %W% %F% %Y% %D% %Q%

# Default relative path for WDIR
WDIR=..

include ../prod/RULES.mi
include ../prod/MAKE.mi

CNAME=maint
IDIR=${IMAGE}/install
OPTDIR=${IMGDIR}/${OPTDIR}
FILES=${IDIR}/INSTALL ${IDIR}/UNINSTALL ${IDIR}/RUN
OPTION=${OPTDIR}/${PROD}.name
SRC=INSTALL.sh UNINSTALL.sh RUN.sh
```

Figure 8.1 Component Makefile for "maint"

---

[3]The component makefiles shown in Figure 8.1 and Appendix E are essentially the same. The only difference is a change in the macro preprocessor used to process the source files.

```
build print clean rmbin::
      @echo "Starting to $@ ${CNAME}

build:: ${FILES} ${OPTION}

print:: prtdate

clean::
      -rm -f idhdr.sh prtdate

rmbin::
      -rm -f ${FILES}

build print clean rmbin::
      @echo "Finished $@ of ${CNAME}

.DEFAULT:
      @echo "No $@ procedure for the ${CNAME} component"

${FILES}: $$(@F).sh ${COMM}/sfmhdr.sh
      ${VC} prodver=${RELNUM} reldate=`date '+%D'` \
            cname=${CNAME} machine=${MACHINE} \
            < ${COMM}/sfmhdr.sh > idhdr.sh
      cat idhdr.sh ${@F}.sh > $@
      chmod ug+x $@
      rm idhdr.sh

${OPTION}: menu.txt
      ${VC} < menu.txt >$@
      chmod 664 $@

include ../prod/PRINT.mi
```

Figure 8.1 Component Makefile for "maint" (Continued)

```
:msg Menu Description for Software Management Menu
:msg %W% %F% %Y% %D% %Q%
Source File Management Package
```

Figure 8.2 Menu Description for List Option

The next task is to modify the product makefile to support this new component (see Figure 8.3 for a list of changes). The maint component must be added to the macro definition for components and package objects. The macro definition for **ETREE** has been expanded to include the new package option directory. Since the package objects in the maint directory are not installed, they should also not be part of the tools directory. By adding a new macro definition (**ITREE**) for an install directory in the image tree, we provide a way that builds the proper package image tree and tools directory. Of course, a new make rule has been added that will build the distribution disk. For the product makefile to execute correctly, the following line must be added to **MAKE.mi**:

OPTDIR=options

```
CMPNTS=common maint sfint scripts
PKGOBJS=maint sfint scripts
ETREE=${IMAGE} ${IMGDIR} ${IMGDIR}/${SFMDIR} ${IMGDIR}/${OPTDIR}
ITREE=${IMAGE}/install

mktool:
        -rm -rf ${TLSDIR}
        WDIR=`dirname \`pwd\``; export WDIR; \
                ${MAKE} ${MFLAGS} image "IMAGE=${TLSDIR}" \
                "IMGDIR=${TLSDIR}" "ITREE="
        WDIR=`dirname \`pwd\``; export WDIR; \
                ${MAKE} ${MFLAGS} install "INSDIR=${TLSDIR}"

mkprod:
        WDIR=`dirname \`pwd\``; export WDIR; \
                ${MAKE} ${MFLAGS} -f Makefile -f FLOPPY.mi mkflop \
                "MNTDIR=install" "OWNER=bin" "GROUP=bin"

image: ${ETREE} ${ITREE}

${ETREE} ${ITREE}:
        mkdir ${MKDFLG} $@
```

Figure 8.3 Modifications to Product Makefile

In the preceding discussion, we are using a floppy disk as the distribution media for the software package. Rather than create another include file, we will modify **FLOPPY.mi** (see Figure 6.10) to include one more target mkflop. As shown in Figure 8.4, the only difference between the save target and mkflop is the changing of owner and group IDs. This change is necessary for the following reasons:

1. The default owner ID and group ID of the image files are a machine-dependent function. For example, the owner and group ID may be "sfm" since this is the name of the package owner. These IDs may or may not exist on another machine.

2. We need to remember that it is the owner or group ID number that is important and not the name. These numbers may already be assigned to another user on another machine.

To make certain that the ownership of the package objects is valid, we assign the owner and group ID a default of "bin". While "bin" is not the only valid choice, the numeric value of "bin" is the same on most machines. Rarely should package objects be owned by "root". This is especially true of SUID programs.

```
xload xsave mkflop::
 .
 .
 .
mkflop::floppy
      ${MOUNT} ${FLPDEV} /${MNTDIR}
      cd ${IMAGE}; find . -depth -print | \
            ${CPIO} -pdmv /${MNTDIR}
      find /${MNTDIR}/${SFMDIR} -depth \
            -exec chown ${OWNER} {} \; \
            -exec chgrp ${GROUP} {} \;
      find /${MNTDIR}/usr/options -depth \
            -exec chown ${OWNER} {} \; \
            -exec chrp ${GROUP} {} \;
      find /${MNTDIR}/install -depth \
            -exec chown ${OWNER} {} \; \
            -exec chgrp ${GROUP} {} \;
 .
 .
 .
xload xsave mkflop::
```

Figure 8.4 Modifications to FLOPPY.mi

This concludes the changes required to implement support for software package maintenance. With just a few changes, we have transformed a software package from a local package to a package that can be installed on any number of machines.

8.3   Software Package Configuration

Whether it is the defining of default printers, communication ports, path names to data files, or any number of other tasks, most software packages have functions that must be done by the system administrator. With these functions goes the question of where to put them. They are not part of the user's functions, and to include them in user's menu both creates unnecessary confusion and opens the door to security violations. But where do the configuration package objects belong?

Prior to UNIX System V Release 2.0, there was no universally accepted method for handling configuration package objects. Starting with Release 2.0, these functions became part of the **sysadm** command's *Package Management* menu. On the surface, this sounds like the perfect solution to the problem. Alas, the solution is not perfect because the entire sysadm menu structure is a creature unto to itself and is not documented. The interface to the *Software Management* option described previously was derived from working through all the related shell scripts; and the interface to *Package Management* was determined by the same technique. In this section, we look at the basic rules for creating an interface to the *Package Management* option.

8.3.1 Package Management Selection Menu

The **sysadm** command takes a unique approach to building its menus. Instead of being based on fixed menus defined within the shell scripts, it uses dynamic menus based on directories. Thus, the directory structure reflects the menu structure. Figure 8.5 shows a portion of the sysadm menu structure that is distributed with SVR3. Although it is not complete, it shows enough to explain how the menu system works.

Thus, one would expect that when the packagemgmt menu option is chosen, the directory names, which are listed in "/usr/admin/menu/packagemgmt", would form the list of menu options. However, a directory name by itself is not sufficient. The directory must contain a file called **DESC**, which, as shown in Figure 8.5, provides the necessary menu information.

Once the option is selected in one menu, another menu is generated from directories names and from shell scripts that contain menu entry identification (discussed more fully later). When a shell script is selected, control is passed to the specified shell script.

Although this process is extremely flexible, it is also a bit slow. The sysadm script actually checks each file in the directory to see if it is to be displayed in the menu. The single advantage to this approach is that the **sysadm** command does not require any changes when an entry is either added or deleted from the menu tree.

8.3.2 Special Syntax for Shell Scripts

The information that separates the shell scripts for the menu system from other shell scripts is contained in three specially formatted comment lines. The format for these lines is

```
#<type># <text>
```

and has the following meanings:

1. *Menu heading:* The **DESC** file contains a line that begins with **#head#** (see Figure 8.6) and is used to define the menu heading for this directory.

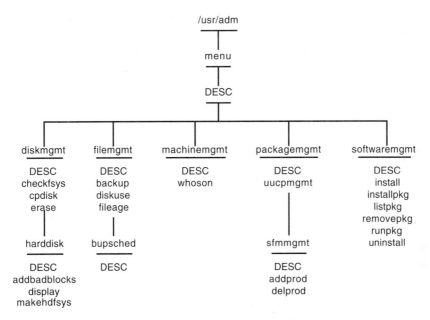

Figure 8.5 Partial of sysadm Menu File Structure

2. *Menu entry description*: Whereas the directory name or file name is used as the menu selector, the description for the menu entry is provided by this line. The line begins with a **#menu#,** followed by a short description of menu option.The **#menu#** line in the **DESC** file (see Figure 8.6) defines the menu description for the parent directory name. However, the **#menu#** line in a shell script (see Figures 8.7 and 8.8) defines the shell script as a menu option and provides the description for the menu entry.

3. *Help message*: Along with each menu option, there is a help message containing one or more lines that begin with **#help#**. Figures 8.6 through 8.8 give examples of how to write such a message.

Using the above three types of lines,[4] we can now write the necessary scripts to interface with the **sysadm** command.

8.3.3 DESC file

Every directory name in the package management directory that includes a **DESC** file is listed as an option in the *Package Management* menu. In essence, the **DESC** file is an extension to the directory name and defines the menu parameters for the directory.

---

[4]The **#ident** line is related to a new way of handling *what strings* and is explained in Chapter 10 when we discuss the **mcs** command.

For example, if the directory */usr/admin/menu/packagemgmt* contained a subdirectory called *sfmmgmt* (see Figure 8.5), the required **DESC** file would be similar to the one shown in Figure 8.6. Using this example, the selection of the Package Management option would display the following:

```
                       PACKAGE MANAGEMENT

1 sfmmgmt        software management menu
2 uucpmgmt       basic networking utilities menu

Enter a number, a name, the initial part of a name, or
? or <number>? for HELP, ^ to GO BACK, q to QUIT:
```

Selection of the **sfmmgmt** option would then result in the display of another menu with the heading

```
          SOURCE   FILE   MANAGEMENT
```

The options would be the shell scripts in the sfmmgmt directory. These shell scripts are discussed in Section 8.3.4.

```
#ident "%W% %F% %Y% %D% %Q%"
#head#                        SOURCE FILE MANAGEMENT
#menu# software management menu
#help#
#help# This menu allows one to create a new interface program
#help# or to delete an existing program. The User ID and
#help# Group Id for the interface program must exist.
```

Figure 8.6   Example of DESC File

8.3.4 Options Menu for the Package

After selecting the option for the package, then what? Since the **sysadm** command only knows how to process menus, it will search the selected directory for scripts that contain **#menu#**. Using Figures 8.7 and 8.8 as examples, these shell scripts will be displayed in a menu as follows:

```
               SOURCE FILE MANAGEMENT

1 addprod          add package to source file management
2 delprod          delete source file interface program

Enter a number, a name, the initial part of a name, or
? or <number>? for HELP, ^ to GO BACK, q to QUIT:
```

When an option is selected, the indicated shell script will be executed. In these examples, the shell scripts will either create or delete the special interface program associated with a software package.

```
#ident "%W% %F% %Y% %D% %Q%"
#menu# add package to source file management
#help#
#help# Before a package can be accessed using the source file
#help# tools, it must have an interface program. This routine
#help# establishes an interface program and sets the user id and
#help# group id. However, the package still must be set up
#help# in the correct format in the Source Library.

flags="-q q -k $$"
SFMDIR="/usr/sfm"

trap exit 1 2 15
trap '  trap "" 1 2 15
       rm -f /tmp/$$*' 0

while true
do
  echo "Enter Package Id: \c"
  read PID
  if [ -z "$PID" ]
  then
    echo '\
Please enter the Package Id that is the name of the directory
in the Source Library that contains the SCCS Source Tree.'
    continue
  fi
  if [ -f $SFMDIR/sfint$PID ]
  then
    echo '\
The interface program for this package already exits.'
    continue
  fi
  break
done

while true
```

Figure 8.7 Add Package Option

```
do
  echo "Enter Owner ID: \c"
  read OWNID
  grep "$OWNID" /etc/passwd > /dev/null && break
  echo "Invalid Owner Id"
done

while true
do
  echo "Enter Group ID: \c"
  read GRPID
  grep "$GRPID" /etc/passwd > /dev/null && break
  echo "Invalid Group ID"
done

cp $SFMDIR/sfintxx $SFMDIR/sfint$PID
chown $OWNID $SFMDIR/sfint$PID
chgrp $GRPID $SFMDIR/sfint$PID
chmod 4710 $SFMDIR/sfint$PID
ln $SFMDIR/sfint$PID $SFMDIR/cdc$PID

echo "Interface program for $PID has been created."
```

Figure 8.7 Add Package Option (Continued)

```
#indent%W% %F% %Y% %D% %Q%"
#menu# delete source file interface program
#help#
#help# Deletes the special interface program for a package from
#help# the source file management directory.

flags="-q q -k $$"
SFMDIR=/usr/sfm

trap exit 1 2 15
trap ' trap "" 1 2 15
      rm -f /tmp/$$*' 0
```

Figure 8.8 Delete Package Interface

```
while true
do
  echo "Enter Package ID: \c"
  read PID
  if [ -z "$PID" ]
  then
    echo "Package Id Required."
    exit 1
  fi
  if [ ! -f $SFMDIR/sfint$PID ]
  then
    echo "Interface program for $PID not found."
    continue
  fi
  break
done

while true
do
  echo "Are you sure you want to delete the Interface for $PID: \c"
  read ANS
  case "$ANS" in
    y|Y) break;;
    n|N) exit;;
    *)   echo "Invalid Answer";;
  esac
done

rm -f $SFMDIR/sfint$PID
rm -f $SFMDIR/cdc$PID
echo "Interface program for $PID removed."
```

Figure 8.8 Delete Package Interface (Continued)

8.3.5 Building Configuration Package Objects

As opposed to the software package maintenance routines described in the first section, the software package configuration routines are a part of the package. They are a subset of the application package object, which alters the configuration of the software package. Therefore, these routines are treated as regular components such as **scripts** or **sfint**. We call this new component **pkgmgmt**. The package objects are built using the makefile shown in Figure 8.9.

Next we need to make a few changes to the product makefile, to **MAKE.mi**, and to **FLOPPY.mi**. First, let's look at the changes to the product makefile:

1. Since we are adding a new component that is part of the software package, we need to modify the definitions of **CMPNTS** and **PKGOBJS** to be as follows:

```
CMPNTS=common maint pkgmgmt sfint scripts
PKGOBJS=maint pkgmgmt sfint scripts
```

2. The new component resides in a different path, so the definition for **ETREE** has to be modified as follows:

```
ETREE=${IMAGE} ${IMGDIR}/${SFMDIR} \
    ${IMGDIR}/${OPTDIR} ${IMGDIR}/admin \
    ${IMGDIR}/admin/menu \
    ${IMGDIR/admin/menu/packagemgmt   \
    ${IMGDIR}/${PRGDIR}
```

For the product makefile, this is all that is needed, because the rest of the makefile is built from these macro definitions. Since the new component will be executed from a different path, this path needs to be defined in **MAKE.mi** by including the following line:

```
PKGDIR=admin/menu/packagement/sfmmgmt
```

If we are also making a distribution disk, we need to add the following lines to the **mkprod** target in **FLOPPY.mi**:

```
find /${MNTDIR}/${PKGDIR} - depth \
    -exec chown ${OWNER} {} \; \
    -exec chgrp ${GROUP} {} \;
```

Finally, the INSTALL and UNINSTALL scripts must be modified to account for the new directory. These changes have already been incorporated into the scripts shown in Appendix E.

```
#   Component Makefile for Source File Management Tools
#
#   Component: pkgmgmt
#
#   %W% %F% %Y% %D% %Q%
#
# Default relative path for WDIR
WDIR=..

include ../prod/RULES.mi
include ../prod/MAKE.mi
```

Figure 8.9 Makefile for Configuration Package Objects

```
CNAME=pkgmgmt
IDIR=${IMGDIR}/${PKGDIR}
PDIR=${IMGDIR}/${PKGDIR}
FILES=${IDIR}/DESC ${IDIR}/addprod ${IDIR}/delprod
INSTF=${PDIR}/DESC ${PDIR}/addprod ${PDIR}/delprod
SRC=DESC.sh addprod.sh delprod.sh

build print clean rmbin::
        @echo "Starting to $@ ${CNAME}

build:: ${FILES}

install:: ${INSTF}

print:: prtdate

clean::
        -rm -f prtdate

rmbin::
        -rm -f ${FILES}

build print clean rmbin::
        @echo "Finished $@ of ${CNAME}

.DEFAULT:
        @echo "No $@ procedure for the ${CNAME} component"

${FILES}: $$(@F).sh
        cp ${@F}.sh $@
        chmod 640 $@

${INSTF}: ${IDIR}/$$(@F)
        ${INSTALL} -f ${@D} -m 640 -u ${OWNER} -g ${GROUP} \
            ${IDIR}/${@F}

include ../prod/PRINT.mi
```

Figure 8.9 Makefile for Configuration Package Objects (Continued)

8.4   Summary

In this chapter, we transformed a software package destined for use on a single machine to one that is an installable package on several machines. By using the *Software Management* option of the **sysadm** command, we eliminated the need for the user to use any special commands to install, remove, or run a package from the distribution media.

We also showed how the *Package Management* menu could be used to simplify the configuration tasks that need to be done from time to time. This objective was accomplished by showing how to add new entries to the *Package Management* menu of the **sysadm** command.

While they are more cumbersome to use, both the software package maintenance and configuration scripts can be used even when the **sysadm** command is not present. However, it makes the job much easier for the system administrator if all software packages can be installed, removed, and maintained through a common interface. Just as we try to improve the human interface for the users of a package, we should try to improve the interface for the system administrator.

Two new components were added to our source tree. The revised source tree is shown in Figure 8.10.

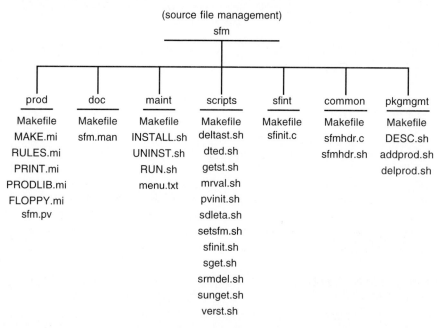

Figure 8.10 Source Tree for Example Software Package

CHAPTER 9

Macro Preprocessors: Making Source More Flexible

9.1 Introduction

There are two choices for managing different renditions[1] of a source file. One is to keep different copies and the other is to use a macro preprocessor. Without going into details, SCCS can manage different versions of a source file by maintaining different branches. Through text substitution, inclusion of external files, and conditional inclusion (or exclusion) of text, a macro preprocessor can create different output files from a single input file.

Which method of rendition management to use depends on several factors. The need for different renditions arises when several machines, or customers, require variations to a common source tree. If all renditions for each new version must be released at once, then using a macro preprocessor is preferred. However, when the release cycles are not linked, maintaining separate branches may be a better solution. Or, perhaps, a combination of the two is required.

How to use SCCS to maintain multiple renditions is the subject of another work.[2] In this chapter, we discuss how to use a macro preprocessor to maintain multiple renditions. Since a macro preprocessor is another software tool used to transform a source file, its integration into the build process is discussed. To accomplish these objectives, we briefly look at what a macro preprocessor is. From this conceptual view of a macro preprocessor, we move to a discussion of the preprocessors available with UNIX System V. To demonstrate the use of macro preprocessors, the header information files in the **common** direc-

---

[1]The term **rendition** is used to distinguish the difference between copies of a source file that have a common ancestor but a different development path (a branch in SCCS terms). The term **version** is used to describe the differences between different generations along a single branch.

[2]For more information on the use of SCCS to manage multiple renditions of a software package, see Israel Silverberg, *Source File Management with SCCS* (Englewood Cliffs, N.J.: Prentice Hall, 1992), Chapter 10.

tory are converted to standard include files and incorporated into the software package as package objects.

9.2   What Is a Macro Preprocessor?

A **macro preprocessor** translates a given input file into a different output file based on the *macro preprocessor command*s embedded in the source file. The macro preprocessor commands control the substitution of text, conditional inclusion or exclusion of text, and the inclusion of other source files. Of course, the macro preprocessor commands are not passed to the output file. The name **macro preprocessor** derives from its use as a front end to an assembler, compiler, interpreter, or text formatter.

9.2.1 String Substitution

When macro preprocessors first appeared, they usually performed a single function: text replacement.[3] The most basic form of *text replacement* took the following form:

```
define {macro name} [{value}]
```

How this form is put into practice varies from one macro preprocessor to another. For purposes of illustration, we will use the **m4** format, which uses the following statement to associate the macro **EOF** with the value of **-1**:

```
define(EOF,-1)
```

With this definition, the macro preprocessor replaces every occurrence of the string **EOF** with a **-1**. This simple technique of text substitution makes a program more readable and easier to modify. Yet it is done without creating a *variable* that would become a part of the data section of an executable program.

An expanded form of text replacement allows for *parameter substitution,* as shown in the following example:

```
define(double(c), (c + c))
```

In this example, the parameter "**c**" will be replaced by an actual value. In other words, the phrase:

```
double(2)
```

---

[3]Brian W. Kernighan and P.J. Plauger, *Software Tools* (Reading, Mass.: Addison-Wesley Publishing Company, 1976), page 251.

will become:

```
(2 + 2)
```

   While text replacement is a useful programming tool, it has no impact on the build process. However, if the macro preprocessor allows for **command line macro definitions**, the build process can alter the resulting source file. For example, the macro facilities of the **make** command are nothing more than a variation of text replacement including command line macro definitions.

9.2.2 Conditional Inclusion or Exclusion

From text replacement, it is but a small step to a **conditional statement**. Although the conditional statement takes on different forms in the various macro preprocessors, the result is the same. The conditional statement allows text to be conditionally included, or excluded, in the output source file.

   For a conditional statement to have a meaning, the macro preprocessor must support command line macro definitions. Now, instead of mere text replacement, we can have **text selection**. This can be very important when building a software package for different environments.

9.2.3 Inclusion of External Files

The inclusion of external files is a programming technique used to define source files that contain statements that may be common to several programs. Examples are the use of **MAKE.mi** and **RULES.mi** in the makefiles that we have written in this book. Another example is the use of ".h" files in 'C' programs.

   Other than modifying a source file, what effect do they have on the build process? The answer is that these files represent the hidden dependencies. In the same manner that the dependency of the object module to its source file forms a relationship, the source file generated by a macro preprocessor is dependent on the files to be included. Thus, a change in any one of these include files may change the final software package. When the include file is within the domain of the software package, it must be listed on the dependency line. When it is external to the software package, it must be part of the version control for software tools.

9.3   UNIX Macro Preprocessors

UNIX does not have one macro preprocessor, it has six: **cpp**, **m4**, **neqn**, **pic**, **tbl**, and **vc**. Because they are more likely to be used with makefiles, three of these (**cpp**, **vc**, and **m4**) are covered in this section. However, the principles discussed in the remainder of this chapter apply to all macro preprocessors.

   Since **cpp** is the more common of the macro preprocessors, it is discussed first. Then we will look at the grandfather of macro preprocessors, **m4**. Finally, we will review the newest macro preprocessor, **vc**. For each macro preprocessor, we need to cover three areas: external definition of macros, use of macros for conditional inclusion or exclusion of text, and the inclusion of external files.

To show how the different macro preprocessors can be used in the build environment, we are going to make another modification to the software package that we have been building. This time the header files in the **common** component are transformed to generic include files. Furthermore, all the necessary macro definitions are passed to the macro preprocessor via the command line.

Of all the changes we have made to the initial software package, this is the most dramatic in that almost every makefile is affected. As a reflection of the new function, the name of the directory for the package header files is changed from **common** to **include**. Because of the number of changes, the revised description files can be found in Appendixes B through H.

9.3.1 "cpp": A Preprocessor for 'C'

The letters "cpp" are an abbreviation of "**C pr**eprocessor." As the name states, it is the macro preprocessor for the 'C' compiler. Rather than providing yet another tutorial on how to use the **cpp** command[4] the following discussion concentrates on how these commands can be used in the build process. This is best accomplished by using the divisions defined previously.

Command Line Macro Definition

With the **-D** option, it is possible either to define or to change the definition of a macro. The format for this option is as follows:

```
-D{name}
-D{name}={definition}
```

On the flip side, the **-U** option can be used to undefine a macro. This option has only one format:

```
-U{name}
```

Setting flags for conditional inclusion or exclusion of text is probably the most common use of the **-D{name}** option. These flags are equivalent to the macro command **#define {name}**.

Usually, the **-D** option allows **cpp** to include compile time constants in the source file. However, there is one major limitation. When it comes to macro substitution within

---

[4]For a detailed discussion of **cpp,** see Samuel P. Harbison and Guy L. Steele, Jr., *C: A Reference Manual* (Englewood Cliffs, N.J.: Prentice Hall, 1987), Chapter 3.

string constants, **cpp** fails miserably. The only way out is to pass the entire string constant to **cpp**.

For example, the **make rule** shown in Figure 9.1 can provide the strings required for the include file shown in Figure 9.2. Notice how this make rule is written. Each string must be quoted because of shell's requirements, and the quotes to be passed as part of the macro definition must be escaped. Using an environmental variable for the current date helps improve readability. Since we are using an environmental variable, the variable name must be escaped to keep **make** from treating it as a macro definition. Also, the option **-D${MACHINE}** defines the hardware type needed for some include files.

```
${IDIR}/sfintxx: $$(@F).c ${IMGDIR}/${INCDIR}/c_stdhdr.h
        RDATE=`date '+%D'`; export RDATE; \
        ${CC} ${CFLAGS} -D${MACHINE} \
        -DSCCS1="\"@(#)${PNAME} for ${OPSYS}/${MACHINE}\"" \
        -DSCCS2="\"@(#)Version: ${RELNUM} Release Date: $$RDATE\"" \
        -DSCCS4="\"@(#)Copyright ${CDATE}. All Rights Reserved.\"" \
        -DSCCS7="\"@(#)Module: ${CNAME}\"" -D${BLDMAC} \
        ${@F}.c -o $@
        chmod 600 $@
```

Figure 9.1 Passing String Constants to cpp

Besides defining macros, it is possible to **undefine** a macro definition with the **-U** option. While it can be used with any macro definition, this option is primarily used to turn off macros used as flags. To get a better picture of how this works, consider a source file that contains the following lines:

```
#define STDBUF

#ifdef STDBUF
#define BUFSIZ 512
#else
#define BUFSIZ 1024
#endif
```

The command

```
$ cc -USTDBUF foo.c
```

changes the BUFSIZ from 512 to 1024.

Conditional Inclusion or Exclusion

A conditional statement begins with an **#if**, **#fidem**, or **#ifndef** command and ends with an **#endif**, **#else**, or **#elif** command. The **#else** or **#elif** commands can also be used to mark the beginning of a statement block. The important point is that *these preprocessor commands bracket one or more statements that will be included or excluded from the output file*.

Figure 9.2 shows an example of how a conditional statement could be used. The **-D${BLDMAC}** macro definition passes the flag value shown in Figure 9.1. The macro **BLDMAC** is defined in **MAKE.mi** and has a default value of **TEST.** If we want to make a final version of the software package, we write the following command:

```
$ make build "BLDMAC=FINAL"
```

This command changes the definition of **BLDMAC**. The new value for **BLDMAC** changes the flag setting and, as a result, the message text to be included in the source file changes.

Inclusion of External Files

In Chapter 5, we saw how we could use include files in makefiles. Similarly, we can define include files in a 'C' source file, and **cpp** will merge the include file into the output source file. During the build process, we can alter the search path for these files. This can be done in one of two ways:

1. Using the **-Y** option, we can change the default *include directory* from /usr/include to another directory. The format of this option varies depending on whether you are executing **cc** or **cpp**. For **cc**, the format is

```
-Y p,{directory name}
```

whereas for **cpp** the format is

```
-Y{directory name}
```

2. We can introduce another directory that is to be searched before searching the default include directory. The format for this option is as follows:

```
-I{directory name}
```

As we saw in Chapter 7, we can use the **-Y** option to specify different versions of the 'C' compiler. In particular, the **-Y I** option controlled the default include directory. Since it alters the include directory search path, the **-I** option serves several purposes, such as the following:

1. One could have a *package include directory* for those include files that are related to the software package. By using the **-I** option, it would not be necessary to specify path names as part of the include file name.

Note: An explicit path name must never be used as part of an include file name. Such a name assumes that the work source tree will always be attached to the same directory. If a path name needs to be specified, it should be a relative path name that does not exceed the bounds of the work source tree.

---

2. We may be using include files that are maintained in the *local include directory*. In keeping with the security guidelines set forth in Chapter 6, we would keep local standard include files separate from those that are distributed with UNIX.

3. When building a software package that has include files that will be a part of either the *default include directory* or *local include directory*, we must use the version of the include files from the package that we are building and not from the installed version.

To see how this works, the software package we have been building needs a few changes. Instead of having a header file that is software package dependent, we can make a universal header file by doing the following:

1. The name for "common" directory changes to "include" directory.

2. The name of the package header file changes from "sfmhdr.c" to "c_stdhdr.h".

3. A few modifications need to be made to the package header file (see Figure 9.2 for the new version).

Once these changes have been made, we have an include file instead of a separate module. To use the new file, we need to add the following line to "sfintxx.c":

```
#include <c_stdhdr.h>
```

Figure 9.1 shows the **make rule** for building **sfintxx**. Notice that the **-I** option is missing. Why? Because we are referring to an include file that should be a part of every software package. Since it is not a part of standard UNIX, it will be part of the *local include directory*, which we will call "/usr/local/include". However, since this software package creates the include file, we cannot refer to the local include directory. Instead, we must refer to the copy in the image directory. This is done by modifying the **CTOOLS** macro in the **RULES.mi** file. The new entry would be as follows:

```
CTOOLS=-Y p,${TLSCCS}/lib -Y 0,${TLSCCS}/lib \
      -Y 2,${TLSCCS}/lib -Y a,${TLSSGU}/bin \
      -Y b,${TLSCCS}/lib -Y 1,${TLSSGU}/bin \
      -Y S,${TLSCCS}/lib -Y I,${TLSCCS}/include \
      -Y L,${TLSCCS}/lib -Y U,${TLSSGU}/lib \
      -I${IMGDIR}/${INCDIR}
```

Of course, the definition for **${INCDIR}** must be added to **MAKE.mi** as follows:

```
INCDIR=local/include
```

Making the new include directory part of the software package is similar to adding any new component. The one difference is that it must be the first component to be built. Appendix C shows the makefile for the new component.

```
/* C Version Header Record for Source Manager */
/* Version: %W%   %F% %Y% %D% %Q% */

/* Macros that must be externally defined
      CDATE=Copyright Date
      CNAME=Component Name
      MACH=Machine Identification
      OPSYS=UNIX System V
      PNAME=Package Name
      PVER=Package Version Number
      RDATE=Release Date

   However, due to cpp's limitations, they must be passed with
   the entire string.
*/

char sccsid1[] = SCCS1;
char sccsid2[] = SCCS2;
char sccsid3[] = "@(#)Uniware, Ltd.";
char sccsid4[] = SCCS4;
#ifdef TEST
char sccsid5[] = "This is a preliminary version.";
#else
char sccsid5[] = "This is a released version.";
#endif
char sccsid6[] = "@(#)\\n";
char sccsid7[] = SCCS7;
```

Figure 9.2 Package Header via an Include File

9.3.2 "m4": The Grandfather of UNIX Macro Preprocessors

Whereas **cpp** is, or will be, bound to the 'C' compiler, **m4** is not bound to any specific language. In fact, it can be used with any text file, be it a program source file or documentation. It is a very flexible and powerful macro preprocessor, which, unfortunately, has receded into relative obscurity. As for **cpp**, we will not present a tutorial on how to use **m4**.[5] Rather, we are going to concentrate on how the build process and **m4** can be integrated. As an example of this integration, we will create a package header file for shell scripts. It should be noted that this discussion only lightly touches the potential capabilities of **m4**.

In this section, we use **m4** as a preprocessor for shell scripts. Unlike other macro preprocessors, **m4** does not have a special prefix to identify a particular token as a macro preprocessor command. For example, **ifdef** in **m4** is **#ifdef** in **cpp**. This creates a few problems in that **shift** and **eval**, which are predefined macros, are also valid shell commands. For a macro preprocessor to be used as a generic preprocessor, it must have some means of resolving such naming conflicts. In **m4**, we can either quote all the occurrences of **eval** and **shift** that we want to be passed to the output or we can rename the predefined macros by using the following commands:

```
define(m4eval,defn(`eval'))
undefine(`eval')
```

The preceding discussion points out another problem, the accent mark and the single quote used by m4 to delineate strings conflict with shell's use of these characters. To get around this problem, we use another predefined macro call, changequote. Figure 9.3 puts all this together as one set of commands that must be at the head of every shell script processed by m4. Since this list is subject to change, we want to ensure that the latest version is always prefixed to a shell script. The m4 command line in Figure 9.4 shows how to use sh_m4def.m4, which contains these macro definitions. This command line takes advantage of the m4 feature in which all input source files are treated as a single file and directed to a single output stream

Command Line Macro Definition

The formats for both defining and undefining macros are the same as for **cpp**. For the software package we have been building, the **m4** command is shown in Figure 9.4. You will notice that there is a major difference between **m4** and **cpp**. Whereas **cpp** does not allow macro substitution within quoted strings, **m4** will perform macro substitution in quoted strings but not in comments. At least in **m4**, there is a way out. As shown in Figures 9.6 and 9.7, we use the **changecom** (change comment delimiters) macro to control macro substitution in comments.

---

[5] For more information on the use of **m4**, see Brian W. Kernighan and Dennis M. Ritchie, "The M4 macro preprocessor," in *UNIX Time Sharing System: UNIX Programmer's Manual,* 7th ed., Volume 2A (Murray Hill, N.J.: Bell Telephone Laboratories, Inc., 1979).

```
dnl(
# Shell m4 Definitions for Source Manager
# Component: include
# Version: %W%   %F% %Y% %D% %Q%

define(meval,defn(`eval'))
undefine(`eval')
define(mshift,defn(`shift'))
undefine(`shift')
changequote(~,~)
)
```

Figure 9.3 m4 Definitions File for Shell Scripts (**sh_m4def.m4**)

```
${FILES}: $$(@F).sh ${IMGDIR}/${INCDIR}/sh_m4def.m4 \
          ${IMGDIR}/${INCDIR}/sh_stdhdr.m4
     ${M4} -DCDATE=${CDATE} -DCNAME=${CNAME} -DMACH=${MACHINE} \
          -DOPSYS="${OPSYS}" -DPNAME="${PNAME}" \
           -DPVER=${RELNUM} -DRDATE=`date '+%D'` \
           -DINC=${IMGDIR}/${INCDIR} -D${BLDMAC} \
           ${IMGDIR}/${INCDIR}/sh_m4def.m4 ${@F}.sh > $@
     chmod +x $@
```

Figure 9.4   Example Make Rule for m4

```
${IDIR}/sfintxx: $$(@F).c ${IMGDIR}/${INCDIR}/c_stdhdr.m4
     ${M4} -DCDATE=${CDATE} -DCNAME=${CNAME} -DMACH=${MACHINE} \
          -DOPSYS="${OPSYS}" -DPNAME="${PNAME}" \
           -DPVER=${RELNUM} -DRDATE=`date '+%D'` \
           -DINC=${IMGDIR}/${INCDIR} \
           ${IMGDIR}/${INCDIR}/c_stdhdr.m4 > c_stdhdr.h
     ${CC} ${CFLAGS} -D${MACHINE} -D${BLDMAC} ${@F}.c -o $@
     chmod 600 $@
     rm c_stdhdr.h
```

Figure 9.5 m4 as a Preprocessor to **cpp**

Using **m4**, we can solve the string substitution problems of **cpp**. The header file is preprocessed by **m4** and then passed to **cpp**. The revised make rule is shown in Figure 9.5. Of course, there are a few caveats. We have to change the default quote marks to prevent substitution within the comments and to force substitution in the SCCS ID strings. Also, we have to undefine the **ifdef** macro to prevent **m4** from processing the **#ifdef** that is meant for **cpp**. These changes are shown in the revised header file (see Figure 9.7). The include statement in the 'C' program must also be changed, as follows, to look for the include file in the correct directory:

```
#include "c_stdhdr.h"
```

Conditional Inclusion or Exclusion

The **ifdef** predefined macro is the basic conditional statement for **m4**. The format for the statement is **ifdef(a,b,c)**, which translates as *if a is defined then b else c*. The third argument is optional and, if not present, has the value of *null*. Following are some examples of valid **ifdef** statements:

```
ifdef(`i386',`define(BUFSIZ,512)',`define(BUFSIZ,1024)')
ifdef(`unix',`define(ISUNIX)')
```

The preceding method works for short text statements (see Figure 9.6 for another example), but does little for deciding whether to include a block of text. One solution is to split the **ifdef** onto multiple lines, as follows:

```
ifdef(`i386',
        `define(BUFSIZ,512)',
        `define(BUFSIZ,1024)')
```

This works but could get a little messy for large blocks of text. In **cpp**, we could define a block of text by using the **#ifdef** and **#endif** commands. In **m4**, the same task would be accomplished in the following manner:

```
ifdef(`i386', divert(-1))
.
.
.
divert(0)
```

Again, **m4** provides many other predefined macros that can be used for text manipulation. A complete discussion of **m4** would require a separate chapter and is beyond the scope of this work.

Inclusion of External Files

With **m4**, we have not one but two predefined macros that can be used to include external files into the source file being processed. The most common macro used is include (file-name). As stated, this format requires the file name to be one of the following:

•In the current working directory

•A relative path name

•An explicit path name

If we want to control the location of the file during the build process, we need to include a macro as part of the file name. The following is an example of how this can be accomplished:

```
define(minclude,defn(`include'))
undefine(`include')
ifdef(`INC',,`define(INC,/usr/local/include)')
minclude(INC/sh_stdhdr.m)
```

In this example, **INC** is not defined in the source file and, if not defined on the **m4** command line, the default will be the "/usr/local/include" directory. A new include directory can be defined by using the following command:

```
m4 -DINC="../image/usr/local/include" foo.sh
```

> **Note:** In the preceding example, the word **include** is part of the directory name and looks like a macro name with no parameters to **m4**. To keep **m4** from processing the directory name as a macro, the macro name had to be redefined. This would be true of any name passed to **m4** that is also a macro name.

Whereas the **include** macro will cause **m4** to abort if the file is not found, the **sinclude** macro will not. One could define the **sinclude** macro as an optional include. In all other respects, it is the same as the include macro.

Back to our software package, Figure 9.6 shows the package header file for shell scripts. To use this header file, each shell script would begin as follows:

```
:
ifdef(~INC~,,~define(INC,/usr/local/include)~)
minclude(INC/sh_stdhdr.m)
```

For this to work, the file **sh_m4def.m4** must precede the shell script file name on the **m4** command line (see Figure 9.4). Also, the redefinition of the **include** macro needs to be added to **sh_m4def. m4** definition file (see Appendix C for a complete definition of this file). Figure 9.7 shows the revised header file for C programs. The make rule in Figure 9.5 illustrates how **m4** processes this header file to create an include file for a C program

```
dnl Shell Version Header Record for Source Manager
dnl
dnl Component: include
dnl
dnl Version: %W% %F% %Y% %D% %Q%
dnl
dnl Macros that must be externally defined
dnl          CDATE=Copyright Date
dnl          CNAME=Component Name
dnl          MACH=Machine Identification
dnl          OPSYS=Operating System
dnl          PNAME=Package Name
dnl          PVER=Package Version Number
dnl          RDATE=Release Date
dnl
changecom()
# @(#)PNAME for OPSYS/MACH
# @(#)Version: PVER  Release Date: RDATE
# @(#)Uniware, Ltd.
# @(#)Copyright CDATE. All Rights Reserved.
ifdef(~TEST~,~# @(#)This is a preliminary version of PNAME.~)
ifdef(~FINAL~,~# @(#)This is a released version of PNAME.~)
# @(#)\\n
# @(#)Module: CNAME
changecom(#)
```

Figure 9.6 Standard Package Header for Shell Scripts

```
changecom(/*,*/)
undefine(`ifdef')
/* C Version Header Record for Source Manager */

/* Component: include */

/* Version: %W%  %F% %Y% %D% %Q% */

/* Macros that must be externally defined
      CDATE=Copyright Date
      CNAME=Component Name
      MACH=Machine Identification
      OPSYS=UNIX System V
      PNAME=Package Name
      PVER=Package Version Number
      RDATE=Release Date

      However, due to cpp's limitations, this header must be
      preprocessed with m4 before passing to cpp.
*/
char sccsid1[] = "@(#)PNAME for OPSYS/MACH";
char sccsid2[] = "@(#)Version: PVER  Release Date: RDATE";
char sccsid3[] = "@(#)Uniware, Ltd.";
char sccsid4[] = "@(#)Copyright CDATE.  All Rights Reserved";
#ifdef TEST
char sccsid5[] = "@(#)This is a preliminary version of PNAME.";
#else
char sccsid5[] = "@(#)This is a released version of PNAME.";
#endif
char sccsid6[] = "@(#)\\n";
char sccsid7[] = "@(#)Module: CNAME";
changecom()
```

Figure 9.7 Package Header File for C Using **m4**

9.3.3 "vc": A Simple Preprocessor

The name **vc** means *version control*, a somewhat misleading name in that the function performed by **vc** is text substitution. Perhaps the name derives from its inclusion in the SCCS tools list.[6] How to use **vc** was fully described in *Source File Management with SCCS*.[7] Since the examples we used prior to this chapter made use of a **vc** processed package header file, we will refer to the appropriate figures.

Command Line Macro Definition

Whether a **keyword** is a macro or a variable is open to debate. However, since the *keyword is replaced by its value*, we will consider it a macro for the purposes of this work. Figures 6.2 and 6.3 show that **vc** uses a slightly different method of parameter passing than was used by either **cpp** or **m4**. The command line format for *assigning values* to keywords is as follows:

```
{keyword=value}
```

The use of the phrase "assigning *values*" is important. Whereas the **-D** option of **cpp** or **m4** was used to define a macro and, optionally, assign a value, in **vc**, a keyword must be defined by the **:dcl** statement. The value for a keyword can either be from the command line or from an **:asg** statement. For our purposes, the following restrictions regarding the uses of keywords are important:

1. Keywords **must** be declared in the source file.

2. Keywords are expected to be assigned a value. A warning message is issued for any keyword that is not assigned a value.

3. The value of a keyword cannot contain any spaces or tabs. In other words, one token is replaced by another token.

4. Keywords in strings or in comments will be replaced when substitution is permitted for the line.

Conditional Inclusion or Exclusion

The **vc** command provides for conditional inclusion or exclusion of text through the use of the **:if** and **:end** statements. There is no **else** statement in **vc**. Thus, when the condition is true, text is passed to standard output. Otherwise, it is skipped. Like **cpp**, the **:if** statement is oriented toward processing one or more lines of text. Using **vc**, our buffer size example might look like the following:

---

[6]AT&T, *UNIX System V: Programmer's Guide* (Englewood Cliffs, N.J.: Prentice Hall, 1987) page 803.

[7]Silverberg, *Source File Management with SCCS*, Chapter 9.

```
:dcl MACH, BUFSIZ
:if :MACH: = i386
:asg BUFSIZ = 512
:end
:if :MACH: != i386
:asg BUFSIZ = 1024
:end
```

Inclusion of External Files

Besides not handling character strings that contain spaces or tabs, the other major weakness of **vc** is that it does not provide any means for including external files into the output source file.

9.4   Macro Preprocessors and makefiles

While macro preprocessors add considerable flexibility to the building of a software package, they do so at a price. In this section, we look at the major problems that must always be considered when using a macro preprocessor.

9.4.1 Macros with External Dependencies

A source file is like a black box, there is nothing on the outside that tells you about the inside. Look at the files shown in Figures 9.6 and 9.7. Each has macros whose definition is external to the file. Moreover, the proper processing of the file depends on those macros being defined. Such definitions can be made on either the macro preprocessor command line or, when include files are used, in an include file.

The problem is not limited to these examples, it is a hidden trap that is buried in many standard include files. For example, the UNIX System V/386 version of stdio.h requires that the type of machine be identified in order for the BUFSIZ macro to be defined, and there is no default. Without careful reading of the include file, this is not apparent. Yet stdio.h is not an exception to the rule. But what is the solution?

In **cpp**, **m4**, and **make**, the use of an undefined macro is perfectly valid and no error or warning messages will be issued. Only **vc** issues a message when a macro is used but not declared or assigned a value. Given such conditions, it is very important for any source file that uses macros with external dependencies to document these dependencies at the beginning of the file. While this approach is subject to all the hazards of source file documentation, it at least gives one a reasonable starting point.

9.4.2 Include Files as Dependencies

Besides the black box problem of not knowing what files are to be included into the output source, there are two other problems. First, should the include file be referenced on the dependency line? Second, when the include file exists in multiple directories, which one is to be used?

Although not an ideal solution, the names of the include files used in a source file can be solved by using the **grep** command to list all the include statements. The great danger lies in nested includes (include statements within include files). A better solution is to use **makedepend** or **maketd**. However, these tools are not included as part of the standard version of UNIX System V.

Once we know what include files are referenced in a source file, we need to decide whether they should be listed on the dependency line. The simplest rule to follow is that *all include files that are part of the software package are referenced on the dependency line; all external include files fall in the sphere of tools management* (see Chapter 7).

As for the second problem, in Chapter 7 we used the **-Y** option to alter the default search path. In this chapter, we showed how we could alter the search sequence for include files with the **-I** option. Because of these options, we have to be very careful that the dependency line and the search paths defined by **cpp** refer to the same file. UNIX does not warn you when the dependency line and command lines are referring to different files. This must be done by manually checking each make rule.

9.5   Summary

Macro preprocessors are powerful tools and are heavily used in the building of any software package. Can you imagine writing a 'C' program or a document without using any macros? It could be done, but it would make the task much more difficult. At the same time, macro preprocessors present special problems to the build process. These problems come as external macro definitions (whether they are used for text substitution or flags for conditional statements) and include files.

In this chapter, we have discussed three of UNIX's macro preprocessors (**cpp**, **m4**, and **vc**) from the following aspects:

•External macro definitions

•Conditional inclusion or exclusion of text

•Inclusion of external files

How preprocessors can be put into practice was illustrated by modifying the software package we have been building. This software package now produces standard package header files that will be placed in the local include directory. This modification also shows us how to handle include files in the build process.

CHAPTER 10

Modifying
the Object File

10.1 Introduction

Although they perform different functions, the commands (**strip**, **cprs**, **conv**, and **mcs**) discussed in this section have one feature in common; each, in some way, modifies the common object file. It may help you to understand the UNIX documentation, but you don't need to be an a.out format expert to understand the information presented in this chapter. Each section will discuss why you might use the command and how you would integrate it into the build process.

10.2   'strip' Command

Unless the **-s** option was passed to **ld** at the time the program was linked, the resulting object file contains a symbol table and line numbering information that is only useful during debugging and testing. Once a program is released, this information becomes excess baggage that only consumes space on disk. The question is how do we keep this information for testing and debugging and remove it when the package is released without having to rebuild the software package, as would be required if we used the **-s** option of the **ld** command.

The **strip** command performs the same function as the **-s** option, but can be executed at any time. Thus, we do not need to make it part of the make rule that compiles the object module. Instead, we can make it part of the make rule that installs the package object. For example, in our software package example, we would modify the install make rule in the component makefile for sfintxx to read as follows:

```
${INSTF}: ${IDIR}/$$(@F)
        ${INSTALL} -f ${@D} -m 600 -u ${OWNER} -g ${GROUP} \
                ${IDIR}/${@F}
        ${STRIP} ${STRPFLG} $@
```

If you are building a distributable version of the software package (see Chapter 8), then the **mkflop** rule in **FLOPPY.mi** must also be modified. Using our example software package, the following line would be added:

```
mkflop: floppy
    .
    .
    .
    ${STRIP} ${STRPFLG} /${MNTDIR}/usr/${SFMDIR}/sfintxx
    .
    .
    .
```

With just a few minor changes, we have removed the symbolic information from the installed package object. This was done without having to build a test version and then turning around and having to build a release version.

10.3   'cprs' Command

The **cprs** command provides another means of reducing the size of the common object file. It accomplishes this by removing all duplicate structure and union descriptors. Given this limited task, there may or may not be a difference between the input file and the output file. In fact, the probability of **cprs** actually reducing the size of the file is very small.

Note: The **cprs** command requires that the symbol table be present. Therefore, it must be executed before the **strip** command and will not work if the **-s** option of the **ld** command was used.

So, if we were to use the **cprs** command, where would it be put? Since it modifies an object file in a way that may affect test results, it needs to be a part of the *build* target. For example, we could modify the sfintxx make rule to be as follows:

```
${IDIR}/sfintxx: $$(@F).c ${IMGDIR}/${INCDIR}/c_stdhdr.m
    .
    .
    .
    ${CC} ${CFLAGS} -D${MACHINE} -D${BLDMAC} ${@F}.c -o $@
    ${CPRS} $@ ${TMP}/${@F}
    mv ${TMP}/${@F} $@
    .
    .
    .
```

However, for **sfintxx**, it would be a wasted effort since it does not contain any duplicate structure or union descriptors.

10.4   'conv' Command

This is truly a very specialized command. Its sole function is to change the byte ordering of the object file to match that of the target machine. So, unless you are cross compiling on a host machine for a target machine, this command is of no value. If you do have a compiler with cross-compilation capability and the target machine uses a byte ordering that is different from the host machine, this command could be placed in the compile make rule.

Actually, the whole area of cross compilation is so fraught with problems that building such a software package is very difficult. It usually implies a split build process with everything up to the building of an image file occurring on the host machine and the remainder of the steps occurring on the target machine. Resolution of these problems is beyond the scope of this work.

10.5   'mcs' Command

mcs is a new command that appeared on the scene with UNIX System V Release 3.0. The name **mcs** stands for "modify **comment section**." The comment section of an object file is used to store comments about the object file and normally has the name **.comment**. The ability to create sections other than the standard **.text**, **.data**, and **.bss** has been around for awhile. So the ability to have a comment section is not new. What is new is the special support given to this section. Let's look at this feature and see how we can use it.

Try the command

```
$ msc -p {object file name}
```

on any object module compiled and linked under UNIX System V Release 3.0 or later. What you get is a long list of *what strings*[1] showing the version of every module linked. But how were these entries created? One way is with the **mcs** command, another way is by using the **#ident** macro of **cpp**. For example, instead of having the line

```
char sccid[] = "%W%   %F% %Y% %D% %Q%";
```

in a 'C' program, we could have the following line:

```
#ident "%W%   %F% %Y% %D% %Q%"
```

---

[1]The **what** command, which is part of the SCCS subsystem, lists all strings in a file that begin with the characters **@(#)**. Thus, the term *what string* refers to any string that begins with these characters. The *what string* is an integral part of the SCCS method of version identification.

Before converting all your *what string*s to the new format, take a moment to consider the implications behind the comment section. The section can be easily modified by anyone who has write permission to the file. Therefore, it is not the best place to store the kind of header information described in Chapter 9. However, it does provide a solution to another problem.

An executable object module is composed of many object modules. To identify the version of the object module, each one should have its own *what string*. This way we can verify that the version of the components of an executable object module are correct. This information is useful during development phase, but in the installed version of the object module, all we care about is the version number of the software package and, possibly, the SCCS ID of the product version file. With the **mcs** command, we keep the package identification and discard the excess information after it is no longer needed.

First, the package header shown in Chapter 9 does not change. This provides the permanent identification information. Second, all SCCS ID strings must use **#ident**. This provides the necessary debugging information. When the distribution media is created or the software package is installed, the contents of the *comments section* are deleted and replaced with comments related to the action taken. For this to make sense, we need to modify some makefiles.

For a locally installed software package, we need to modify the install make rule to read as follows:

```
${INSTF}: ${IDIR}/$$(@F)
        ${INSTALL} -f ${@D} -m 600 -u ${OWNER} \
             -g ${GROUP} ${IDIR}/${@F}
        ${STRIP} ${STRPFLG} $@
        ${MCS} -d \
          -a "@(#)Installed on `date '+%D at %T'`." $@
```

In this **mcs** command, we deleted the contents of the *comments section* (the **-d** option) and then appended a new comment (the -**a** option). We can also use it to identify when the distribution floppy was created by making the following modifications to **FLOPPY.mi**.

```
mkflop: floppy
     .
     .
     .
     ${STRIP} ${STRPFLG} /${MNTDIR}/usr/${SFMDIR}/sfintxx
     ${MCS} -d -a "@(#)Distribution disk created on \
      `date '+%D at %T'`." \
      /${MNTDIR}/usr/${SFMDIR}/sfintxx
     .
     .
     .
```

The install script (**INSTALL.sh**) can also be modified to log the date that **sfintxx** was installed. We just need to add the following lines after the routine that changes the group and owner IDs of the installed files:

```
# update executable files to show date installed
mcs -a "@(#)Installed on `date '+%D at %T'`." \
  /usr/sfm/sfintxx
```

In this example, we only append a new comment to the list of existing comments. Using the preceding techniques, the comments section can serve both debugging and event logging functions.

10.6   Summary

In this brief chapter, we discussed how we would incorporate the utilities that modify the object file into the build process. Of the commands covered, **strip** and **mcs** should be used whenever object files are being built. The **strip** command reduces the size of an installed object file. The **mcs** can be used to remove *what strings* that are useful for debugging and to add *what strings* that reflect changes in the status of the installed object file. Although the **cprs** and **conv** commands also modify the object file, their use is limited to special cases.

CHAPTER 11

Building
a Library File

11.1   Introduction

As we saw in Chapter 5, the building and maintenance of an **archive library file** are different from any other type of file. Since it is a collection of many individual files collected into a single file, an archive library file may consist of object files, data files, source files, or any mixture of these. In this chapter, we are concerned only with the building, maintenance, and use of an archive library file that is exclusively composed of nonexecutable object files. In other words, we are restricting ourselves to the archive library file used by the *link editor* to build another object file.

Starting with UNIX System V Release 3.0, another form of library file came into being, the **shared library file**. The essence of the shared library notion is that instead of statically binding the object modules at compile time to the output object module, the object modules are dynamically loaded at the time of execution. It is beyond the scope of this book to explain the shared library concept in detail. For this information, read the appropriate chapters in the *Unix System V: Programmer's Guide*.[1] In this work, our concern is limited to showing how to build a shared library file.

The examples in this chapter are composed of functions from the program **sfintxx**. In choosing which functions were to be a part of the library, consideration was given to whether the function could be used in another application program. The bigger question of whether these functions should be a part of the software package we are building or should be a part of another software package is beyond the scope of this book.

---

[1]AT&T, *UNIX System V: Programmer's Guide* (Englewood Cliffs, N.J.: Prentice Hall, 1987), p. 291.

11.2   How to Reference a Library File

Before we can build and use an archive library file, we need to review how library files are referenced by the *link editor*. Unless the link-editing phase is suppressed via the **-c**, **-E**, **-P**, or **-S** options of the **cc** command, the *link editor* (**ld**) attempts to resolve all external references contained in the object modules that are being linked. This is done by processing the object modules in the order given on the command line, with the library **libc.a** being the last place searched.

> **Note:** An object file or library is processed only once. If a later object file library has a reference that would have been resolved in a previously specified library, it is left unresolved. Thus, the order in which the object files and libraries are specified is very important.

To specify an archive library file, we use the syntax

```
-l{library name}.
```

The **{library name}** is translated into a file with the name of **lib{library name}.a**. For example, the command line option of **-lm** would be taken to refer to the library file called **libm.a**.

Which search path is used by the *link editor* to find this library file? The answer to this question is implementation dependent. In general, **ld** looks first at the directory called **LIBDIR** and then in **LLIBDIR**. The normal default locations for these directories are "/lib" and "/usr/lib", respectively. As we saw in Chapter 7, the values for **LIBDIR** and **LLIBDIR** can be changed with the **-Y** option.

Another directory can be added to the search path via the **-L** option. To affect the search path, this option must be specified before the library name. For example, we could reference a library in a local library directory with the following command:

```
$ cc example.c -L /usr/local/lib -lsfm
```

This command causes **ld** to look in "/usr/local/lib" before looking in **LIBDIR** or **LLIBDIR**. It is possible to reference a library in yet another directory by repeating the **-L** option. Thus, we could have a command line that looks like

```
$ cc example.c -L /usr/tlib -lx -L /usr/local/lib -lsfm
```

Using a shared library is not unlike using any other library. Since there will normally be an archive library companion to the shared library, the shared library must be referenced first. Thus, any references not resolved by the shared library would be resolved by the archive library. For example, the command line

```
$ cc example.c -lnsl_s -lnsl
```

causes the shared network library to be referenced before the archive network library.

> **Recommendation!** If your system supports **shared libraries**, use them. The reduction in size of the object files is amazing.

The preceding information is useful in any situation where one needs to use a library that is located in other than the default directories. The rest of the chapter is important to those who need to build a library file.

11.3   Building an Archive Library

When one thinks of a library, it is usually in terms of the libraries provided as part of a language software package (libc.a, libm.a, and the like) or as part of the tools provided to interface to an application software package (libnls.a libwindows.a). Rarely does one think of a library as a useful tool in building a software package or for providing a standardized library of reusable object modules. Yet these are valid reasons for building an archive library. Before discussing how to build a library file, let's look more closely at the reasons for building one.

The first category of libraries is a **distributed archive library** and includes both libraries that are part of language and application libraries. The important feature of these libraries is that they are part of the distributed software package. Since this is the most comprehensive form of library file, it is used in our examples.

The second category of libraries is the **package archive library**. This is the library file that is used in building a software package, but it is not part of the distributed package. Why build a library file when any object file needed as part of an executable object file can be specifically referenced on the command line? For object modules that are only used by a single component, there is no reason. However, here are three reasons (and there are probably more) for object files that are used by several components:

1. Writing the command line becomes easier in that only the library has to be referenced and not every object file. Also, the dependency line can be changed to reference the library instead of individual object files. This may seem like a bit of overkill, but the following should make this a little clearer.

2. It is one way to solve the problem of always having to make changes to a makefile when a reference to a new library function is made within the source file.

3. In addition, one does not have to figure out how to reference indirect changes. That is, object module x.o references y.o and y.o changes, but not x.o. If a program uses a function declared in x.o and has even listed x.o as a dependency, it would not be considered out of date if there was a change to y.o.

The last category of library file is the **common archive library**. As programmers, we seem to be afflicted with the disease of having to reinvent the wheel every time we write a new program. Instead of rewriting functions, if they were part of a common archive library, we could reuse them. This would save much of the time spent in thinking, writing, and testing functions that are used repeatedly. In a sense, it is taking those functions already in the package archive library that can be used in more than one software package and placing them in a library that is available to all software packages. The common archive library is different from a distributed archive library in that it does not support a particular software package.[2]

Now that we understand some of the reasons for a library, let's look at how we go about building one.

11.3.1 Preparing the Source File

As part of the creation of any library file, you should create a corresponding include file. At a minimum, this include file should contain the declarations of the data type returned for every function in the library that could be referenced by another object module. Thus, two purposes are served by the include file. First, it ensures that the data type for the function is correctly declared. Second, it defines those functions in the library that are available for reference. For example, the include file might contain the following statements:

```
char    *funca()            /* explanation */
void    funcb()             /* explanation */
```

The library might also contain a **funcx( )** that is used by **funca( )** and **funcb( )** but is not useful as an independent function.

In addition, the include file should take care of any standard macro definitions, typedef statements, and external references. The goal is that the user of the library should not have to guess about what is needed to correctly use it.

> **Note:** Clearly, a function in a library should avoid any reference to global variables. A good library function only makes reference to the arguments given and provides an optional return value.

When you link a function like **execvp( )** to another object module, are you linking the function or the entire object module, which contains other **exec** functions? If your answer was that the function was linked, you are wrong. The entire object module, of which **execvp( )** is a part, is linked. In practical terms, this means that each object module in a library should be composed of one function or, at least, a small group of tightly bound functions. One function per object module is preferable since it ensures that no unused object modules are linked with another object module.

---

[2]Management of the transfer of an object module from a package archive library to a common archive library should be made as simple as possible. For example, once a software package has been developed and tested, any candidates for inclusion could be submitted as a *change request* to the manager of the common archive library. He or she would review the submission and, if accepted, would incorporate it into the common archive library.

Appendix D shows examples of source files for a library file. Appendix C shows the include file for this library file. While the include file is technically a part of the source for the library, we put it in the include directory so that all include files are in one location. Besides adding the file to the "include" component, all we have to modify in the "include" makefile is the FILES, INSTF, and SRC macro definitions.

11.3.2 Creating a Library Component

By this time, creating a new component, which will be called *lib*, should be an automatic process. In this section, we are only going to concentrate on the make rules required to build and install the library. The remaining make rules are so generic that no changes are required to them.

What are we building and installing? It is a library file, so the macro definitions reference the library file and not the object modules that are included within it. Thus, the macro definitions are as follows:

```
FILES=${IDIR}/libsfm.a
INSTF=${PDIR}/libsfm.a
```

But the library file is dependent on its components, so we use the following make rule to define this relationship:

```
${IDIR}/libsfm.a:  ${IDIR}/libsfm.a(libhdr.o) \
                   ${IDIR}/libsfm.a(substr.o)
```

From this, we are ready to define the make rules for building each object module that makes up a library. The first module, **libhdr.o**, is a compiled version of the file **c_stdhdr.m4** and provides the means to place the package identification header into the library. The make rule for this is as follows:

```
${IDIR}/libsfm.a(libhdr.o): ${IMGDIR}/${INCDIR}/c_stdhdr.m4
include ../prod/M4SHDR.mi
            ${IMGDIR}/${INCDIR}/c_stdhdr.m4 > libhdr.c
    ${CC} -c ${CFLAGS} -D${MACHINE} -D${BLDMAC} ${%:.o=.c}
    ar ${ARFLAGS} $@ $%
    rm libhdr*
```

Generally, we should use an inference rule to make the remaining components. However, the requirement that both the **{from suffix}** and the **{to suffix}** be in the same directory (see Section 5.4.7) prevents the use of such a rule. So we will write explicit make rules as follows:

```
${IDIR}/libsfm.a(substr.o): substr.c
    ${CC} -c ${CFLAGS} -D${MACHINE} -D${BLDMAC} ${%:.o=.c}
    ar ${ARFLAGS} $@ $%
    rm $%
```

The process defined so far for building a library does not consider the order of the library. Since the **ld** command will make multiple passes over a library to resolve all external references, having the library ordered is not necessary. However, when the library contains many object modules that have external references to other object modules within the same library, some speed improvement in the link edit phase can be achieved by ordering the library file.

This ordering is accomplished by using the **lorder** and **tsort** commands. The problem is how to implement these commands. Ideally, one would build all the modules, order them, and then build the library file based on the defined order. This may work perfectly fine if we always build the library from scratch, but what happens if we are only replacing object modules in the library? Unfortunately, with **lorder** and **tsort**, there is no nice neat solution to the problem.[3]

The last task to be dealt with is the installation of the library into a production directory if it is a distributed archive library or a common archive library. We will start with the standard install procedure as defined in Section 10.5 and see what has to be changed.

Since this is an archive library containing linkable object modules, we cannot strip the static symbol information, the external symbol information, or the relocation information. However, information such as the line number information can be removed. To accomplish this, the **strip** command needs to be executed with the **-r** option. While removing the unwanted information, the **strip** command also destroys the archive symbol table, which then has to be rebuilt with the **ar** command.

The real question is what to do with the **mcs** command. We really only want to update the comments section of the **libhdr.o** module. We do not want to remove the *what strings* from the remaining object modules in the library or add the install information to these object modules. Alas, when processing an archive library, the **mcs** command performs the defined operations on all object modules in the file. The only way to modify a single module is to extract it from the library, modify it, and then return it. To avoid this messy operation, we will opt for an intermediate solution by not removing any information and just appending the install information.

Combining the **strip** and **mcs** changes, we have the following make rule for installing a library:

```
${INSTF}: ${IDIR}/$$(@F)
        ${INSTALL} -f ${@D} -m 664 -u ${OWNER} -g ${GROUP} \
            ${IDIR}/${@F}
        -${STRIP} -r $@
        ${MCS} -a "@(#)Installed on `date '+%D at %T'`." $@
        ar ts $@
```

Of course, FLOPPY.mi, INSTALL.sh, and UNINSTALL.sh have to be modified to incorporate these changes (see Appendix E).

---

[3]Although it is not part of the standard version of UNIX, **ranlib** provides a better mechanism for ordering and reordering archive libraries.

11.4   Building a Shared Library

The shared library idea is a relatively new one to the UNIX collection of software development tools. Whether you are building a distributed archive library, a package archive library, or a common archive library, you should consider the possibility of building a companion shared library. If you have routines that meet the qualifications,[4] the savings in disk space and memory space are well worth the effort.

When we speak of a shared library, we are actually speaking about two libraries. When an executable object is link edited, it will use the host shared library. This library provides all the necessary pointers that are needed by the run-time library called the target shared library. An important feature of the shared library is the ability to update the target shared library without recompiling the object files. As we shall see, achieving this goal requires some planning.

While these are not the best examples of shared library functions, the functions used to build the archive library are used to show how to create a shared library. In keeping with the conventions used by UNIX for shared libraries, a shared library will be identified by appending '_s' to the library name. So, in this section, we will build a host shared library (the library used in the link editing) called **libsfm_s.a** and a target shared library (the library used during execution) called **libsfm_s**.

11.4.1   Preparing the Source File

One benefit of a shared library is that any changes made to the target library automatically affect the next execution of a program that uses that shared library function. For example, if **substr( )** were changed, **sfintxx** would not have to be recompiled to reflect the change. However, this benefit does not come without a price. The price is that all external references must be constant from version to version. For this to occur, we must follow a few rules.

> **Rule 1:** *Avoid the use of global variables.*

As stated before, functions should be self-contained modules. The problem is that many, if not most, 'C' compilers treat any data declaration that does not occur within a function to be an external global variable. If we follow the rule that each object module should contain only one function, then there should never be a need to define a variable outside the function. Within a function, we must explicitly state that the variable is **extern** for it to be considered a global variable.

---

[4]For more information on how to choose library members, see AT&T, *UNIX System V: Programmer's Guide*, p. 318.

The source files that we are using in this section (see Appendix D) do not contain any external global variables.

> **Rule 2:** *When used, global variables must be in a separate object module.*

This is a defensive tactic used when external global variables are unavoidable. By keeping the global variables in a separate file, we keep the address of the variable constant from one version to the next.

> **Rule 3:** *Initialize all global variables in the file in which they are defined.*

Failure to follow this rule may result in the link editor altering the address of the variable.

11.4.2 Resolving Symbols External to the Library

A basic assumption of a shared library is that all symbols are resolved within the library. The problem is that most shared libraries will refer to functions that are external to the library and, occasionally, to variables that are external to the library. Details about how to handle these issues are provided in the *UNIX System V: Programmer's Guide*. From our perspective, it means that we must consider another include file (extsym.h) and another object file (p_strlen.c). See Appendix D for more details about these files. What is important is the impact they have on the build process.

If we are to build both an archive library and a shared library, we need to modify **sfintxx.c** (see Appendix H) to only include **extsym.h** when building the *shared library*. This also means that the object modules that are to be added to the archive library are different from those that make up the shared library. Not only are the individual object modules different, but the shared library may not contain all the modules that are in the archive library, and the archive library will not contain the object modules required for external references. Thus, although the source files may be similar, the build process is substantially different.

11.4.3 "mkshlib" Command

Once all the source files have been modified, we are ready to create a shared library by using the **mkshlib** command. The **mkshlib** command is very straightforward. Based on the parameters given in the specification file, the **mkshlib** command will create the host shared library and the target shared library. It all sounds very simple, but there are a few catches that will complicate this simple task.

The **mkshlib** command only builds the host shared library and target shared library. It does *not* update them! Furthermore, the complicated nature of the members of the library prohibits the normal use of the **ar** command to update the library. This means a change to any member of the library will force the library to be created from scratch. Also, since we do not want to mix object modules for an archive library with those for a shared library, we must remove all the object modules after a library is built. Thus, all the object modules that are to be included in the shared library must be recompiled even if only one has changed.

The specification file required by **mkshlib** also presents a problem. Throughout this work, we have tried to maintain a hardware-independent environment. Yet the address declarations required in the specification file are strictly hardware dependent. To get around this problem, we will use **m4** to preprocess the file.

The resulting make rule required to build a shared library looks like the following example:

```
${IDIR_S}/libsfm_s: ${SHSRC} extsym.h libsfm.sl
     ${CC} ${CFLAGS} -c -D${MACHINE} -D${BLDMAC} \
          -DSHLIB ${SHSRC}
     m4 -D${MACHINE} libsfm.sl > t_libsfm.sl
     ${MKSHLIB} -s t_libsfm.sl -t $@ \
          -h ../image/usr/${LIBDIR}/${@F}.a
     rm ${SHSRC:.c=.o} t_libsfm.sl
```

Several items should be noted about this make rule. First, although there are two output package objects, only one is the target. This works because both package objects are built simultaneously. To simplify the use of suffixes, the target shared library was chosen as the target for the make rule. Second, in the version of **mkshlib** used in the preparation of this book, the **-h** assumed that the host shared library would always be built in the same directory as the source files. To get around this limitation, we had to specify the path as a relative path. This problem may or may not exist on other versions of **mkshlib**.

Installing a shared library is a little different from installing an archive library. The host shared library is like an archive library and is installed in the same manner. However, the target shared library is more closely akin to an a.out file and, therefore, uses the same install procedure. Full details for the procedures are contained in the appropriate appendixes.

11.5   Summary

Using libraries other than the 'C' library is a fairly common occurrence. We first showed how to reference additional libraries and how to alter the default library file search path.

For those who need to build an archive library, we next covered the issues involved in this task. As we saw, given well-written source files, the building of an archive library is not a complicated process.

The last section of the chapter discussed the shared library, which is a new feature of UNIX starting with Release 3.0 of UNIX System V. Although building a shared library is a more complicated task than building an archive library, the resulting savings in storage and memory requirements may make the additional work well worth the effort.

CHAPTER 12

Epilogue

12.1   A Review

In Chapter 1, we presented the problems in building a software package. From this discussion, we decided that our prime objective was to be able to build this software package repeatedly and always achieve the same results. Using the formula

```
source files + tools + build instructions = software package
```

we quickly reviewed the UNIX solution to this equation in Chapter 2.

In the next three chapters, we discussed the many features of the **make** command. In Chapter 6, we turned from the details of the **make** command to a practical application of what we had learned. We covered all the topics necessary to build the software package presented in Chapter 1. At this point, we had all the information necessary to build and install most software packages on a local machine.

In Chapter 7, we showed how to change the software package from one that was based on the installed development tools to an environment in which the tools are also a controlled part of the build process. With this change, we made it possible to ensure that the binary image could be re-created at any time.

To many programmers, the idea of building an installable software package is a worry confined to the world of software houses. However, in today's world, it is altogether possible that an in-house software package may be installed on more than one machine. In Chapter 8, we showed how to build such a package.

In Chapter 9, we showed how macro preprocessors could be used to modify the input source file. Now, we can use the same source files and build process to create different renditions of the software package. Well, if you can modify the input, you can also modify the output. This was the topic of Chapter 10.

In Chapter 11, we learned how to use and build both archive libraries and shared libraries. Although archive libraries are old hat to the world of UNIX, shared libraries represent a new feature that was introduced with Release 3.0 of UNIX System V.

12.2   The New Software Package

In Chapter 1, we said that one core example would be used throughout the book. This example was the Source File Management source files as shown in Figure 1.4. This group of source files has been changed and molded into a software package that is installable from a distribution media, builds standardized include files, and provides both an archive library and shared library version of several functions that may be useful in the development of other software packages. From the work source tree diagram shown in Figure 1.4, the package has changed to the work source tree shown in Figure 12.1.

In each chapter, we modified the software package a little here and a little there. In Appendixes B through H, all these changes are brought together to give the complete set of files needed to build the new and revised package. Although these files are used to build a specific software package, they are sufficiently generic to be used as models for other software packages.

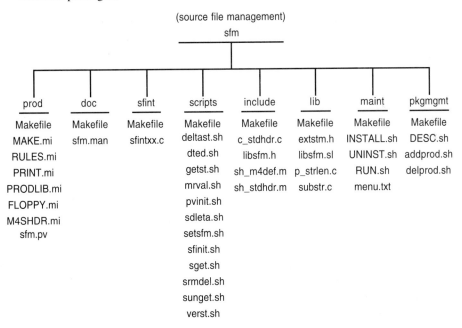

Figure 12.1 Revised Work Source Tree

12.3   Relationship to Source File Management

In *Source File Management with SCCS,*[1] an approach to source file management based on the existence of a source file library was presented. With the tools presented (the tools that we used as examples in this work), we were able to have complete control over the revision history of a software package. With this work, we have expanded our capability to be able to reliably reproduce any version of a software package.

By combining the tools presented in both works, a developer can extract a software package from the source file library, make any necessary changes, build the package, and save any changes back into the library. The configuration management group, or equivalent, could extract the identical set of files using a specific set of tools and build an identical binary image of the software package.

Although this is not the end of the story in the software development cycle, it does provide a solid basis for the management of any software package.

---

[1]Israel Silverberg, *Source File Management with SCCS* (Englewood Cliffs, N.J.: Prentice Hall, 1992).

APPENDIX A

Default Definitions for "make"

```
TZ = PST
TERM = vt100
PATH = /bin:/usr/bin:/etc:/usr/sfm::
MAIL = /usr/mail/pgmr1
LOGNAME = pgmr1
HOME = /u/pgmr1
```

```
YFLAGS =
YACC = yacc
LDFLAGS =
LD = ld
LFLAGS =
LEX = lex
GFLAGS =
GET = get
F77FLAGS =
F77 = f77
CFLAGS = -O
CC = cc
ASFLAGS =
AS = as
ARFLAGS = rv
AR = ar
MAKE = make
$ = $
MAKEFLAGS = b
```

```
.h~.h:
      $(GET) $(GFLAGS) $<


.s~.a:
      $(GET) $(GFLAGS) $<
      $(AS) $(ASFLAGS) -o $*.o $*.s
      $(AR) $(ARFLAGS) $@ $*.o
      -rm -f $*.[so]


.c~.a:
      $(GET) $(GFLAGS) $<
      $(CC) -c $(CFLAGS) $*.c
      $(AR) $(ARFLAGS) $@ $*.o
      rm -f $*.[co]


.c.a:
      $(CC) -c $(CFLAGS) $<
      $(AR) $(ARFLAGS) $@ $*.o
      rm -f $*.o


.l.c:
      $(LEX) $(LFLAGS) $<
      mv lex.yy.c $@


.y~.y:
      $(GET) $(GFLAGS) $<


.y~.c:
      $(GET) $(GFLAGS) $<
      $(YACC) $(YFLAGS) $*.y
      mv y.tab.c $*.c
      -rm -f $*.y


.y.c:
      $(YACC) $(YFLAGS) $<
      mv y.tab.c $@


.l~.o:
      $(GET) $(GFLAGS) $<
      $(LEX) $(LFLAGS) $*.l
      $(CC) $(CFLAGS) -c lex.yy.c
      rm -f lex.yy.c $*.l
      mv lex.yy.o $*.o
```

```
.l~.l:
      $(GET) $(GFLAGS) $<


.l~.c:
      $(GET) $(GFLAGS) $<
      $(LEX) $(LFLAGS) $*.l
      mv lex.yy.c $@
      -rm -f $*.l


.l.o:
      $(LEX) $(LFLAGS) $<
      $(CC) $(CFLAGS) -c lex.yy.c
      rm lex.yy.c
      mv lex.yy.o $@


.y~.o:
      $(GET) $(GFLAGS) $<
      $(YACC) $(YFLAGS) $*.y
      $(CC) $(CFLAGS) -c y.tab.c
      rm -f y.tab.c $*.y
      mv y.tab.o $*.o


.y.o:
      $(YACC) $(YFLAGS) $<
      $(CC) $(CFLAGS) -c y.tab.c
      rm y.tab.c
      mv y.tab.o $@


.sh~.sh:
      $(GET) $(GFLAGS) $<


.s~.s:
      $(GET) $(GFLAGS) $<


.s~.o:
      $(GET) $(GFLAGS) $<
      $(AS) $(ASFLAGS) -o $*.o $*.s
      -rm -f $*.s


.s.o:
      $(AS) $(ASFLAGS) -o $@<
```

```
.f~.o:
        $(GET) $(GFLAGS) $<
        $<F77) $(F77FLAGS) $(LDFLAGS) -c $*.f
        -rm -f $*.f

.f~.f:
        $(GET) $(GFLAGS) $<

.f~.a:
        $(GET) $(GFLAGS) $<
        $(F77) $(F77FLAGS) $(LDFLAGS) -c $*.f
        $(AR) $(ARFLAGS) $@ $*.o
        -rm -f $*.[fo]

.f.o:
        $(F77) $(F77FLAGS) $(LDFLAGS) -c $*.f

.f.a:
        $(F77) $(F77FLAGS) $(LDFLAGS) -c $*.f
        $(AR) $(ARFLAGS) $@ $*.o
        -rm -f $*.o

.c~.o:
        $(GET) $(GFLAGS) $<
        $(CC) $(CFLAGS) -c $*.c
        -rm -f $*.c

.c~.c:
        $(GET) $(GFLAGS) $<

.c.o:

        $(CC) $(CFLAGS) -c $<

.f~:
        $(GET) $(GFLAGS) $<
        $(F77) $(F77FLAGS) $(LDFLAGS) $< -o $*
        -rm -f $*.f

.f:
        $(F77) $(F77FLAGS) $(LDFLAGS) $< -o $@
```

```
.sh~:
      $(GET) $(GFLAGS) $<
      cp $*.sh $*; chmod 0777 $@
      -rm -f $*.sh

.sh:
      cp $< $@; chmod 0777 $@

.c~:

      $(GET) $(GFLAGS) $<
      $(CC) $(CFLAGS) $(LDFLAGS) $*.c  -o $*
      -rm -f $*.c

.c:
      $(CC) $(CFLAGS)  $(LDFLAGS) $< -o $@
```

Default .SUFFIXES

```
.SUFFIXES: .o .c .c~ .y .y~ .l .l~ s .s~ .h .h~ .sh .sh~ .f .f~
```

APPENDIX B

Product Component: "prod"

Component

prod

Description

The product makefile controls actions performed on the entire software package. The action targets are as follows:

build   Build software package and place objects in image directory.

install   Install software package on local machine.

mktool   Install in Tools Library.

mkprod   Create a Distribution Diskette.

print   Print the source files that have changed since the last execution of this target.

lint   Check C source files with lint.

clean   Remove extraneous work files.

rmbin   Remove objects from image directory.

load   Load image directory from Product Library (default) or from floppy disk (LDSAV=FLOPPY.mi).

save   Save copy of image directory in Product Library (default) or on floppy disk (LDSAV=FLOPPY.mi).

For the build, clean, lint, print, and rmbin targets, the default is to perform the selected action on all the components. This can be changed by giving a new definition for the CMPNTS macro. For the install, mktool, and mkprod targets, the action applies to the components defined by the PKGOBJS macro.

Which version line to use in the Package Identification Header is defined by BLD-MAC. The default definition is TEST. This can be changed to FINAL.

Examples

$ make build
$ make build CMPNTS=sfint
$ make build BLDMAC=FINAL
$ make install
$ make install PKGOBJS=sfint
$ make save LDSAV=FLOPPY.mi

Files

Besides the product makefile, this component contains all the make include files for the software package. These make include files can be divided into two categories: product makefile extensions and common include files.

Product Makefile Extensions:

     FLOPPY.mi, PRODLIB.mi

Common Include Files

     M4SHDR.mi, MAKE.mi, PRINT.mi, RULES.mi

This component also contains the product version file: sfm.pv.

Source

Except for sfm.pv, which is not created by the user, all the source files for this component are listed in this appendix.

File Name: Makefile

```
#   Product Makefile for Source File Management Tools
#
#   %W% %F% %Y% %D% %Q%
#
```

```
#  Provide relative definition for WDIR that is required in MAKE.mi
WDIR=..

include RULES.mi
include MAKE.mi

CMPNTS=include lib maint pkgmgmt sfint scripts
PKGOBJS=include lib maint pkgmgmt sfint scripts
ETREE=${IMAGE} ${IMGDIR} ${IMGDIR}/${SFMDIR} ${IMGDIR}/${INCDIR} \
      ${IMGDIR}/${LIBDIR} ${IMGDIR}/${SHLDIR} \
      ${IMGDIR}/${OPTDIR} ${IMGDIR}/admin ${IMGDIR}/admin/menu \
      ${IMGDIR}/admin/menu/packagemgmt ${IMGDIR}/${PKGDIR}
ITREE=${IMAGE}/install
MFLAGS=-e
LDSAV=PRODLIB.mi

help:
        @echo "This is the Master Makefile for ${PNAME}."
        @echo "Following is a list of valid action targets:"
        @echo "  build   - build package and place in image directory"
        @echo "  install - install on local machine"
        @echo "  mktool  - install in Tools Library"
        @echo "  mkprod  - create distribution diskette"
        @echo "  print   - print source files"
        @echo "  lint    - check C source files with lint"
        @echo "  clean   - remove work files"
        @echo "  rmbin   - remove files from image directory"
        @echo "  load    - load image directory from previous version"
        @echo "             LDSAV defines include to be used for both"
        @echo "             load and save.  The default is PRODLIB.mi."
        @echo "  save    - make copy of image directory"
        @echo "build, clean, lint, print, and rmbin can be made for:"
        @echo "  ${CMPNTS}"
        @echo "The install, mktool, and mkprod targets can be made for:"
        @echo "  ${PKGOBJS}"
        @echo "For example, to build the component sfint use this line"
        @echo "  make build CMPNTS=sfint"
        @echo
        @echo "The Package Idenfication string will change depending on"
        @echo "the value of BLDMAC.  The valid values for BLDMAC are"
        @echo "TEST (default) and FINAL.

build load:: image

build::
        @echo "**** The value of BLDMAC is ${BLDMAC} ****"
```

```
build clean lint print rmbin::
        for i in ${CMPNTS}; do \
                (WDIR=`dirname \`pwd\``; export WDIR; \
                eval `tail -1 ${WDIR}/.sfmdata`; \
                umask ${UMODE}; cd $$WDIR/$$i; ${MAKE} ${MFLAGS} $@); \
        done

install: build
        for i in ${PKGOBJS}; do \
                (WDIR=`dirname \`pwd\``; export WDIR; \
                eval `tail -1 ${WDIR}/.sfmdata`; \
                umask ${UMODE}; cd $$WDIR/$$i; ${MAKE} ${MFLAGS} $@); \
        done

load save::
        WDIR=`dirname \`pwd\``; export WDIR; \
                ${MAKE} ${MFLAGS} -f Makefile -f ${LDSAV} x$@

mktool:
        -rm -rf ${TLSDIR}
        WDIR=`dirname \`pwd\``; export WDIR; \
                ${MAKE} ${MFLAGS} image "IMAGE=${TLSDIR}" \
                "IMGDIR=${TLSDIR}" \
                "ITREE="
        WDIR=`dirname \`pwd\``; export WDIR; \
                ${MAKE} ${MFLAGS} install "INSDIR=${TLSDIR}"

mkprod:
        WDIR=`dirname \`pwd\``; export WDIR; \
                ${MAKE} ${MFLAGS} -f Makefile -f FLOPPY.mi mkflop \
                "MNTDIR=install" "OWNER=bin" "GROUP=bin"

.DEFAULT:
        ${MAKE} ${MFLAGS} help

image: ${ETREE} ${ITREE}

${ETREE} ${ITREE}:
        -mkdir ${MKDFLG} $@
```

Notes to Product Makefile

1. For the macro definitions in MAKE.mi to have precedence over RULES.mi, the include lines must be specified in the order shown.

2. The CMPNTS macro should list all components. The PKGOBJS macro defines only those components that are package objects.

3. To ensure that the user always specifies the action target, the default target is help.

4. The build and load, for example, show how the double-colon option of the **make** command is implemented.

5. By simply changing the reference for the install directory, it is possible for the mktools target to install the package in a version-controlled directory.

6. The mkprod target shows how we can concatenate different makefiles and still keep the same targets.

7. The .DEFAULT target traps any invalid name typed on the command line and displays the help target.

8. To build an image tree, we first need to make each directory a dependency of a dummy target. The directory names are also target names for a make rule that actually creates the directory.

9. The load, save, mktool, and mkprod targets show how to define a new environment and then reexecute the same makefile.

File Name: FLOPPY.mi

```
#   floppy make rule
#   %W% %F% %Y% %D% %Q%
#
#   The following macros are defined in the Makefile
#
CPIO=cpio
FORMAT=format
FMTFLG=
LABELIT=labelit
MKFS=mkfs
MOUNT=mount
UMOUNT=umount

FLPBLK=2048
FLPCYL=32
FLPDEV=/dev/dsk/f0q15dt
FLPGAP=2
FLPIND=256
FLPLBL=${PROD}${RELNUM}
FLPRDEV=/dev/rdsk/f0q15dt
MNTDIR=mnt
```

```
xload:
        ${MOUNT} ${FLPDEV} /${MNTDIR}
        cd /${MNTDIR}; find . -depth -print | \
                ${CPIO} -pdmv ${IMAGE}
        ${UMOUNT} ${FLPDEV}


xsave: floppy
        ${MOUNT} ${FLPDEV} /${MNTDIR}
        cd ${IMAGE}; find . -depth -print | \
                ${CPIO} -pdmv /${MNTDIR}
        ${UMOUNT} ${FLPDEV}


mkflop:floppy
        ${MOUNT} ${FLPDEV} /${MNTDIR}
        cd ${IMAGE}; find . -depth -print | \
                ${CPIO} -pdmv /${MNTDIR}
        find /${MNTDIR}/usr/${SFMDIR} -depth \
                -exec chown ${OWNER} {} \; \
                -exec chgrp ${GROUP} {} \;
        ${STRIP} ${STRPFLG} /${MNTDIR}/usr/${SFMDIR}/sfintxx
        ${MCS} -d -a "@(#)Package disk created on `date '+%D at %T'`." \
                /${MNTDIR}/usr/${SFMDIR}/sfintxx
        find /${MNTDIR}/usr/${LIBDIR} -depth \
                -exec chown ${OWNER} {} \; \
                -exec chgrp ${GROUP} {} \;
        -${STRIP} -r /${MNTDIR}/usr/${LIBDIR}/libsfm.a \
                    /${MNTDIR}/usr/${LIBDIR}/libsfm_s.a
        ${MCS} -a "@(#)Package disk created on `date '+%D at %T'`." \
                /${MNTDIR}/usr/${LIBDIR}/libsfm.a \
                /${MNTDIR}/usr/${LIBDIR}/libsfm_s.a
        ${AR} ts /${MNTDIR}/usr/${LIBDIR}/libsfm.a
        ${AR} ts /${MNTDIR}/usr/${LIBDIR}/libsfm_s.a
        find /${MNTDIR}/usr/${SHLDIR} -depth \
                -exec chown ${OWNER} {} \; \
                -exec chgrp ${GROUP} {} \;
        ${STRIP} ${STRPFLG} /${MNTDIR}/usr/${SHLDIR}/libsfm_s
        ${MCS} -d -a "@(#)Package disk created on `date '+%D at %T'`." \
                /${MNTDIR}/usr/${SHLDIR}/libsfm_s
        find /${MNTDIR}/usr/${INCDIR} -depth \
                -exec chown ${OWNER} {} \; \
                -exec chgrp ${GROUP} {} \;
        find /${MNTDIR}/usr/${OPTDIR} -depth \
                -exec chown ${OWNER} {} \; \
                -exec chgrp ${GROUP} {} \;
        find /${MNTDIR}/usr/${PKGDIR} -depth \
                -exec chown ${OWNER} {} \; \
                -exec chgrp ${GROUP} {} \;
        find /${MNTDIR}/install -depth \
```

```
        -exec chown ${OWNER} {} \; \
        -exec chgrp ${GROUP} {} \;
    ${UMOUNT} ${FLPDEV}
floppy:
    @echo 'Insert Floppy Disk in Drive 0, then type <ENTER>'
    @line > /dev/null 2>&1
    @echo 'Formatting Distribution Disk'
    ${FORMAT} ${FMTFLG} ${FLPRDEV}
    ${MKFS} ${FLPRDEV} ${FLPBLK}:${FLPIND} ${FLPGAP} ${FLPCYL}
    ${LABELIT} ${FLPRDEV} ${MNTDIR} ${FLPLBL}
```

Notes to FLOPPY.mi

1. By defining all of the floppy-disk-related macros in this file, it is possible to have several such include files for different floppy formats.

2. The xload and xsave targets are for the loading and saving of the image directory.

3. The mkflop target shows how to build a floppy disk that can be distributed to other machines.

4. Both xsave and mkflop require a formatted floppy disk. The floppy make rule shows how this could be implemented in a makefile.

File Name: PRODLIB.mi

```
#   prodlib make rule
#   %W% %F% %Y% %D% %Q%
#
#   Requires that the following macros be defined in the Makefile
#
CPIO=cpio

PRDLIB=/prodlib

xload:
    cd ${PRDLIB}/${PROD}/${RELNUM}; \
        find . -depth -print | \
        ${CPIO} -pdmv ${IMAGE}


xsave: ${PRDLIB}/${PROD} ${PRDLIB}/${PROD}/${RELNUM}
    cd ${IMAGE}; find . -depth -print | \
        ${CPIO} -pdmv ${PRDLIB}/${PROD}/${RELNUM}


${PRDLIB}/${PROD} ${PRDLIB}/${PROD}/${RELNUM}:
    mkdir -m 770 $@
    chgrp ${GROUP} $@
    chown ${OWNER} $@
```

Notes to PRODLIB.mi

1. Like FLOPPY.mi, this include file is used to load and save a copy of the software package image.

2. Since we are not creating an external media, this include file does not have a target that is equivalent to mkflop.

File Name: M4SHDR.mi

```
#   Standard m4 Command Line Used to Build Source Management Tools
#   %W% %F% %Y% %D% %Q%
    ${M4} -DM4CDATE=${CDATE} -DM4CNAME=${CNAME} -DM4MACH=${MACHINE} \
        -DM4OPSYS="${OPSYS}" -DM4PNAME="${PNAME}" -DM4PSID=${PSID} \
        -DM4PVER=${RELNUM} -DM4RDATE=`date '+%D'` \
```

Notes to M4SHDR.mi

1. This include file standardizes the passing of macros to **m4** for the processing of the package identification header.

2. Blank lines are not permitted because this include file is part of a make rule.

3. The input and output to **m4** are not defined and are to be part of the line following the include file.

File Name: MAKE.mi

```
#   Make Variables Used to Build Source Management Tools
#   %W% %F% %Y% %D% %Q%

# Shell Macro Definitions
PATH=/bin:/usr/bin:/etc:/usr/sfm:
SHELL=/bin/sh
UMODE=022

# Package Macro Definitions
BLDMAC=TEST
CDATE=1990
GROUP=local
MACHINE=i386
OPSYS=UNIX System V
OWNER=local
```

```
PNAME=Source Manager
PROD=sfm
RELNUM=1.3

# Root Directory Macro Definitions
IMAGE=${WDIR}/image
IMGDIR=${IMAGE}/usr
INSDIR=/usr
TLSDIR=/tls/sfm/${RELNUM}

# Package Directory Macro Definitions
INCDIR=local/include
LIBDIR=local/lib
OPTDIR=options
PKGDIR=admin/menu/packagemgmt/sfmmgmt
SFMDIR=sfm
SHLDIR=local/shlib

# Local Definitions
INCSFM=${IMGDIR}/${INCDIR}
LIBSFM=${IMGDIR}/${LIBDIR}
```

Notes to MAKE.mi

1. MAKE.mi is used to define the software-package-related macros. To make the file more readable, the macros are divided into groups.

2. The **MACHINE** macro must represent a valid machine as defined in **stdio.h**. For example, for UNIX System V Release 3.0, the valid machines are u370, vax, u3b, M32, u3b15, u3b5, u3b2, i286, i386, and pdp11.

3. The release number referred to in the **RELNUM** macro is the software package version number. As such, it will change with each new release of the software package. In some cases, the prerelease version may have a different number than the final version (for example, the prerelease versions for release 1.1 would be 1.1a, 1.1b, and so forth).

4. The *root directory macro definitions* define the different base directories for the executable image of the package. With this approach, we have one standard executable image that is attached to different points.

5. The *package directory macro definitions* define the tree for the executable image.

6. For lack of a better name, the *local definitions* category refers to any include or library paths that are neither package directory macro definitions nor part of the definition for controlled software tools.

File Name: PRINT.mi

```
#  Print Make Rule Used to Build Source Management Tools
#  %W% %F% %Y% %D% %Q%
#
#  Requires that the following macros be defined in the Makefile
#     SRC=list of source files
#
.PRECIOUS: prtdate

prtdate: ${SRC}
        pr ${PRFLAGS} $? | lp ${LPFLAGS}
        touch $@
```

Notes to PRINT.mi

1. The special target **.PRECIOUS** protects the file **prtdate** from being erased when **make** terminates abnormally.

File Name: RULES.mi

```
#  Make Rules Used to Build Source Management Tools
#
#  %W% %F% %Y% %D% %Q%

# definition of special tools directories
TLSCCS=
TLSSFM=/tls/sfm/1.1
TLSSGU=

# definition of libraries
SHLIB=-lc_s

# definition of tools
AR=${TLSSGU}/bin/ar
AS=${TLSSGU}/bin/as
ASFLAGS=
ASTOOLS=-Y m,${M4}
CC=${TLSCCS}/bin/cc
CFLAGS=-O
CTOOLS=-Y p,${TLSCCS}/lib -Y 0,${TLSCCS}/lib \
       -Y 2,${TLSCCS}/lib -Y a,${TLSSGU}/bin \
       -Y b,${TLSCCS}/lib -Y 1,${TLSSGU}/bin \
       -Y S,${TLSCCS}/lib -Y I,${TLSCCS}/usr/include \
       -Y L,${TLSCCS}/lib -Y U,${TLSSGU}/lib
```

```
GET=${TLSSFM}/bin/sget
INSTALL=${TLSSGU}/etc/install
LD=${TLSSGU}/bin/ld
LDFLAGS=
LDTOOLS= -Y L,${TLSCCS}/lib -Y U,${TLSSGU}/lib
LEX=${TLSSGU}/usr/bin/lex
LINT=/usr/bin/lint
LTFLAGS=
M4=${TLSSGU}/usr/bin/m4
MAKE=${TLSSGU}/bin/make
MCS=${TLSSGU}/usr/bin/mcs
MKDFLG=-p -m 775
MKSHLIB=${TLSSGU}/bin/mkshlib
SFLAGS=
STRIP=${TLSSGU}/bin/strip
STRPFLG=
VC=${TLSSGU}/usr/bin/vc


.SUFFIXES: .ln

.c.ln:
        ${LINT} ${LTFLAGS} -c -D${MACHINE} -D${BLDMAC} \
             -I${IMGDIR}/${INCDIR} $<


# disable default rules related to SCCS
.sh~.sh:;


.c~.o:;


.c~.c:;


.sh~:;


.c~:;
```

Notes to RULES.mi

1. The aim of this makefile is to define all the software tools that actively affect the package objects. By having explicit control over the tools used, it is possible to ensure that, with the exception of the dates in the *what strings*, the binary image of the package object remains constant. For convenience, RULES.mi is divided into several sections.

2. In the first section, we declared what version of controlled tools is to be used. This section is present only when version control is applied to software tools.

3. Every software tool is given an explicit path name and, if it is a controlled software tool, the macro for the tools library is also specified.

4. The last section in the file contains all the specification for inference rules. Explicit make rules should never be part of RULES.mi, because the first explicit make rule becomes the default rule for the makefile.

APPENDIX C

Include Component: "include"

Component

include

Description

The *include* makefile controls actions performed on the include component. The action targets are as follows:

build   Build component and place package objects in image directory.

install   Install package objects on local machine.

mktool   Not implemented at component level.

mkprod   Not implemented at component level.

print   Print the source files that have changed since the last execution of this target.

lint   Not implemented in this component.

clean   Remove extraneous work files.

rmbin   Remove package objects from image directory.

load   Not implemented at component level.

save   Not implemented at component level.

The default is to execute the **build** target.

Examples

$ make
$ make build

Files

Besides the component makefile, this component contains all the installable include files for the package. These include files can be divided into two categories as follows:

Package Header Include Files:

c_stdhdr.m4, sh_m4def.m4, sh_stdhdr.m4

Library Include File:

libsfm.h

Source

All the source files for this component are listed in this appendix.

File Name: Makefile

```
#   Component Makefile for Source File Management Tools
#
#   Component: include
#
#   %W% %F% %Y% %D% %Q%
#

# Default relative path for WDIR
WDIR=..

include ../prod/RULES.mi
include ../prod/MAKE.mi

CNAME=include
IDIR=${IMGDIR}/${INCDIR}
PDIR=${INSDIR}/${INCDIR}
FILES=${IDIR}/c_stdhdr.m4 ${IDIR}/sh_stdhdr.m4 ${IDIR}/sh_m4def.m4 \
      ${IDIR}/libsfm.h
INSTF=${PDIR}/c_stdhdr.m4 ${PDIR}/sh_stdhdr.m4 ${PDIR}/sh_m4def.m4 \
      ${PDIR}/libsfm.h
```

```
SRC=c_stdhdr.m4 sh_stdhdr.m4 sh_m4def.m4 libsfm.h

build install print clean rmbin::
        @echo "Starting to $@ ${CNAME}"

build:: ${FILES}

install:: ${INSTF}

print:: prtdate

clean::
        -rm -f prtdate

rmbin::
        -rm -f ${FILES}

build install print clean rmbin::
        @echo "Finished $@ of ${CNAME}"

.DEFAULT:
        @echo "No $@ procedure for the ${CNAME} component"

${FILES}: $$(@F)
        cp ${@F} $@
        chmod 644 $@

${INSTF}: ${IDIR}/$$(@F)
        ${INSTALL} -f ${@D} -m 755 -u ${OWNER} -g ${GROUP} ${IDIR}/${@F}

include ../prod/PRINT.mi
```

Notes to Include Makefile

1. Although it could be added easily, the component makefile does not contain a dummy target for help message.

2. The .DEFAULT target merely declares that the procedure does not exist. This simple information message is tied to the product makefile, where it is desirable to know what action has been taken by each component.

File Name: c_stdhdr.m4

```
changecom(/*,*/)dnl
undefine(`ifdef')dnl
/* C Package Header Record for Source Manager */

/* Component: include */

/* Version: %W%  %F% %Y% %D% %Q% */

/* Macros that must be externally defined
      M4CDATE=Copyright Date
      M4CNAME=Component Name
      M4MACH=Machine Identification
      M4OPSYS=UNIX Syste V
      M4PNAME=Package Name
      M4PSID=Package Version File ID
      M4PVER=Package Version Number
      M4RDATE=Release Date

   Due to cpp's limitations, this header must be preprocessed
   with m4 before passing to cpp.
*/

static char sccsid1[] = "@(#)M4PNAME for M4OPSYS/M4MACH";
static char sccsid2[] = "@(#)Version: M4PVER  Release Date: M4RDATE";
static char sccsid3[] = "@(#)Uniware, Ltd.";
static char sccsid4[] = "@(#)Copyright M4DATE.  All Rights Reserved";
#ifdef TEST
static char sccsid5[] = "@(#)This is a preliminary version of M4PNAME.";
#else
static char sccsid5[] = "@(#)This is a released version of M4PNAME.";
#endif
static char sccsid6[] = "@(#)Product Version File: M4PSID";
static char sccsid7[] = "@(#)\\n";
static char sccsid8[] = "@(#)Module: M4CNAME";
changecom()dnl
```

Notes to c_stdhdr.m4

1. By first processing the file through **m4**, it is possible to circumvent **cpp**'s inability to perform macro substitution within strings.

2. The integrity of the C comments is preserved by changing the comment delimiters to those used by C.

3. The *ifdef* macro of **m4** must be undefined so as not to conflict with **cpp**.

File Name: sh_m4def.m4

```
dnl(
# Shell m4 Definitions for Source Manager

# Component: include

# Version: %W%   %F% %Y% %D% %Q%

define(meval,defn(`eval'))
undefine(`eval')
define(minclude,defn(`include'))
undefine(`include')
define(mshift,defn(`shift'))
undefine(`shift')
changequote(~,~)
)
```

Notes to sh_m4def.m4

1. If a line only contains a macro definition, the **m4** command will still send the
    newline to the output. By using the *dnl* macro, these blank lines can be elimi-
    nated from the output. This particular file does not contain any lines that need to
    go to standard output, so one *dnl* macro can bracket the entire file.

2. The standard **m4** quotation marks are in conflict with the quotations marks used
    in shell files. So as not to alter the shell commands, we must change the quote
    marks to a sequence that is not used by shell.

3. Some of the **m4** predefined macros have names that are the same as those of shell
    commands or names used in macro definitions. By defining a new name, we can
    still use the **m4** macro.

File Name: sh_stdhdr.m4

```
dnl(
# Shell Version Header Record for Source Manager
#
# Component: include
#
# Version: %W% %F% %Y% %D% %Q%
#
# Macros that must be externally defined
#      M4CDATE=Copyright Date
#      M4CNAME=Component Name
```

```
#       M4MACH=Machine Identification
#       M4OPSYS=Operating System
#       M4PNAME=Package Name
#       M4PSID=Package Version File ID
#       M4PVER=Package Version Number
#       M4RDATE=Release Date
#
changecom()
)
# @(#)M4PNAME for M4OPSYS/M4MACH
# @(#)Version: M4PVER  Release Date: M4RDATE
# @(#)Uniware, Ltd.
# @(#)Copyright M4CDATE.  All Rights Reserved.
dnl(
ifdef(~TEST~,~define(M4NOTE,~This is a test version of M4PNAME.~)~)
ifdef(~FINAL~,~define(M4NOTE,~Thisisareleasedversionof M4PNAME.~)~)
)
# @(#)M4NOTE
# @(#)Product Version File: M4PSID
# @(#)\\n
# @(#)Module: M4CNAME
dnl(changecom(#))
```

Notes to sh_stdhdr.m4

1. Just as **cpp** does not perform macro substitution within quoted strings, **m4** does not perform macro substitution within comments. However, for the shell version of the package header, we need to perform substitution within comments. Since the section is rather short, we solve this problem by canceling comment delimiters and then restoring them when we are finished.

2. While the *dnl* macro suppresses blank lines on the output, it also throws all characters from the macro through the newline character. To get around this problem, the strings defined by the *ifdef* macros had to become macro definitions for *M4NOTE*.

File Name: libsfm.h

```
/* libsfm.a Header Record for Source Manager */

/* Component: include */

/* Version: %W%  %F% %Y% %D% %Q% */

/* function declarations */
int    substr();/* get substring s1 from s2 from pos x to y */
```

Notes to libsfm.h

1. This header file is to be included in any program that uses either the libsfm.a or libsfm_s.a library.

APPENDIX D

Library Component: "lib"

Component

lib

Description

The library makefile controls all actions involved in the building and installing of the archive library, shared library, and lint file for the archive library. The action targets are as follows:

build	Build component and place objects in image directory.
install	Install package objects on local machine.
mktool	Not implemented at component level.
mkprod	Not implemented at component level.
print	Print the source files that have changed since the last execution of this target.
lint	Check C source files with lint.
clean	Remove extraneous work files.
rmbin	Remove files from image directory.
load	Not implemented at component level.
save	Not implemented at component level.

The default is to execute the **build** target.

Examples

$ make
$ make build

Files

Besides the component makefile, this component contains the files used to build the archive library and shared library. In addition, a lint library is built for the archive library. These files can be divided into two categories as follows:

Archive Library File:

      substr.c

Shared Library Files:

      extsym.h, libsfm.sl, p_strlen.c

Source

All the source files for this component are listed in this appendix.

File Name: Makefile

```
#   Component Makefile for Source File Management Tools
#
#   Component: lib
#
#   %W% %F% %Y% %D% %Q%
#

# Default definition for WDIR
WDIR=..

include ../prod/RULES.mi
include ../prod/MAKE.mi

CNAME=lib
IDIR=${IMGDIR}/${LIBDIR}
PDIR=${INSDIR}/${LIBDIR}
IDIR_S=${IMGDIR}/${SHLDIR}
PDIR_S=${INSDIR}/${SHLDIR}
FILES=${IDIR}/libsfm.a ${IDIR}/llib-lsfm.ln ${IDIR_S}/libsfm_s
```

```
INSTF=${PDIR_S}/libsfm_s
INSTL=${PDIR}/libsfm.a ${PDIR}/libsfm_s.a
INSTLN=${PDIR}/llib-lsfm.ln
SHSRC=p_strlen.c substr.c
SRC=p_strlen.c substr.c
LINTF=${SRC:.c=.ln}

build install lint print clean rmbin::
        @echo "Starting to $@ ${CNAME}"

build:: ${FILES}

install:: ${INSTL} ${INSTLN} ${INSTF}

lint:: ${LINTF}
        ${LINT} ${LTFLAGS} ${LINTF}

print:: prtdate

clean::
        -rm -f *.o *.ln prtdate libhdr.c

rmbin::
        -rm -f ${FILES} ${IDIR}/libsfm_s.a

build install lint print clean rmbin::
        @echo "Finished $@ of ${CNAME}"

.DEFAULT:
        @echo "No $@ procedure for the ${CNAME} component"

${IDIR}/libsfm.a${IDIR}/libsfm.a(libhdr.o${IDIR}/libsfm.a(substr.o)

${IDIR}/libsfm.a(libhdr.o): ${INCSFM}/c_stdhdr.m4
include ../prod/M4SHDR.mi
            ${INCSFM}/c_stdhdr.m4 > libhdr.c
        ${CC} -c ${CFLAGS} ${CTOOLS} -D${MACHINE} -D${BLDMAC} \
            -I${INCSFM} ${%:.o=.c}
        ${AR} ${ARFLAGS} $@ $%
        rm libhdr*

${IDIR}/libsfm.a(substr.o): substr.c extsym.h
        ${CC} -c ${CFLAGS} ${CTOOLS} -D${MACHINE} -D${BLDMAC} \
            -I${INCSFM} ${%:.o=.c}
        ${AR} ${ARFLAGS} $@ $%
        rm $%

# The lint library must always be built from scratch
```

```
${IDIR}/llib-lsfm.ln: ${SRC} extsym.h
        ${LINT} ${LTFLAGS} -uxvo sfm ${SRC}
        mv llib-lsfm.ln ${IDIR}

# The host library option of mkshlib requires a relative path name.
# This is not a documented feature.
${IDIR_S}/libsfm_s: ${SHSRC} extsym.h libsfm.sl
        ${CC} ${CFLAGS} ${CTOOLS} -c -D${MACHINE} -D${BLDMAC} -DSHLIB \
                -I${INCSFM} ${SHSRC}
        ${M4} -DTDIR=${INSDIR}/${SHLDIR}/libsfm_s -D${MACHINE} \
                libsfm.sl > t_libsfm.sl
        ${MKSHLIB} -st_libsfm.sl -t $@ -h ../image/usr/${LIBDIR}/${@F}.a
        rm ${SHSRC:.c=.o} t_libsfm.sl

${INSTL}: ${IDIR}/$$(@F)
        ${INSTALL} -f ${@D} -m 664 -u ${OWNER} -g ${GROUP} ${IDIR}/${@F}
        -${STRIP} -r $@
        ${MCS} -a "@(#)Installed on `date '+%D at %T'`." $@
        ${AR} ts $@

${INSTLN}: ${IDIR}/$$(@F)
        ${INSTALL} -f ${@D} -m 664 -u ${OWNER} -g ${GROUP} ${IDIR}/${@F}

${INSTF}: ${IDIR_S}/$$(@F)
        ${INSTALL} -f ${@D} -m 775 -u ${OWNER} -g ${GROUP} ${IDIR_S}/${@F}
        -${STRIP} -r $@
        ${MCS} -d -a "@(#)Installed on `date '+%D at %T'`." $@

include ../prod/PRINT.mi
```

Notes to Library Makefile

1. The IDIR and PDIR macros define the archive library and the host shared library directories. The IDIR_S and PDIR_S macros define the directories for the target shared library.

2. The FILES macro is used to define the package objects that are to be built in this makefile. However, in the case of a shared library, both the host and target libraries are built at the same time by the **mkshlib** command. Therefore, only one of the files can be defined as the package object to be built.

3. In this component, we must have different install procedures for each type of library file being created. This is reflected in the three different INST macros (INSTF, INSTL, and INSTLN).

4. In this makefile there is no difference between the macros SHSRC and SRC. Under normal conditions, the files listed in SHSRC would be a subset of those defined by SRC.

5. For the archive library (libsfm.a), we can limit the build to just the modules that have changed in the library. The makefile also shows how a package header could be added to the archive library.

6. Building a lint library is not a piecemeal task. If one module changes, we rebuild the entire library.

7. The **mkshlib** command does not provide for updating a shared library. Like the lint library, the shared library must always be built from scratch.

8. The UNIX System V Release 3.0 version of the **mkshlib** command will allow an absolute path name to be given for the target shared library. However, the host shared library can only be placed in another directory by a relative path name.

9. The **m4** command is used to preprocess the shared library definition file. Using this technique, we can use one library for different machines.

10. The **mcs** command cannot update just one module in a library. Instead, it will update the comment section in every module.

File Name: extsym.h

```
/* extsym.h - Header file for external symbols */

#ident "%W% %F% %Y% %D% %Q%"

/* Macro definitions needed to import symbols */

#define strlen(*_libsfm_strlen)
```

Notes to extsym.h

1. This header file defines the external symbols that are referenced by the modules in the library. This file is required only when building a shared library. Also, since it is only related to the building of the library, it does not need to be placed in the include component.

File Name:libsfm.sl

```
changecom(`##')
undefine(`substr')
## libsfm.sl - Specification file for shared library

#ident "%W% %F% %Y% %D% %Q%"
```

```
#target TDIR

ifdef(`u3b2',`#address .text 0x80580000')
ifdef(`u3b2',`#address .data 0x805a0000')

ifdef(`i286',`#address .text 0x16f00000')
ifdef(`i286',`#address .data 0x17f00000')

ifdef(`i386',`#address .text 0xaa000000')
ifdef(`i386',`#address .data 0xaa400000')

#branch
        substr          1

#objects
        p_strlen.o
        substr.o

#init substr.o
        _libsfm_strlenstrlen
```

Notes to libsfm.sl

1. For the shared library specification file, the '##' is used to delimit a comment. The **changecom** macro is used to define the change to **m4**.

2. Once again, we have a conflict between an **m4** macro and a token defined in the source file. Since we have no need for the substr macro, we will just undefine it.

File Name: p_strlen.c

```
/* p_strlen.c - initialization routine for pointer to strlen */

#ident "%W% %F% %Y% %D% %Q%"

#include "extsym.h"

int (*_libsfm_strlen)() = 0;
```

Notes to p_strlen.c

1. A shared library requires that external symbols be referenced via a pointer. This file establishes the pointer for the *strlen* function.

File Name: substr.c

```c
/* substr.c - Routine to select substring from string */

#ident "%W% %F% %Y% %D% %Q%"

#ifdef SHLIB
#include "extsym.h"
#endif

#include <string.h>

/* Select a substring from str2 starting at bpos to epos
 * and put results int str1. Return length of string.
 */

int substr(str1, str2, bpos, epos)
char    *str1, *str2;
int     bpos, epos;
{
        int     i, j;

        if (epos <= bpos)
                str1[0] = '\0';
        else {
                j = 0;
                for (i = bpos; i < epos; i++)
                        str1[j++] = str2[i];
                str1[j] = '\0';
        }
        return(strlen(str1));
}
```

Notes to substr.c

1. All the other files in this component were created to place this one module in a
   shared library. While an actual library would have many more functions, this
   module demonstrates what is required to build an archive library or a shared
   library.

2. The SHLIB macro is used to define whether the module is to be built for an
   archive library or a shared library. For a shared library, we need to replace a call
   to a function by a pointer to the function.

APPENDIX E

Maintenance Component: "maint"

Component

maint

Description

The maintenance makefile builds, but does not install, the software maintenance package objects. The action targets are as follows:

build   Build component and place objects in image directory.

install   Not implemented for this component.

mktool   Not implemented at component level.

mkprod   Not implemented at component level.

print   Print the source files that have changed since the last execution of this target.

lint   Not implemented for this component.

clean   Remove extraneous work files.

rmbin   Remove objects from image directory.

load   Not implemented at component level.

save   Not implemented at component level.

The default is to execute the **build** target.

Examples

$ make
$ make clean

Files

Besides the component makefile, this component contains all the shell scripts that are necessary to support the *Software Management Option* of the **sysadm** command. These scripts are as follows:

> INSTALL.sh, UNINSTALL.sh, RUN.sh

In addition, a special menu entry, "sfm.name," is built from the "menu.txt" file.

Source

All the source files for this component are listed in this appendix.

File Name: Makefile

```
#   Component Makefile for Source File Management Tools
#
#   Component: maint
#
#   %W% %F% %Y% %D% %Q%
#

# Default definition for WDIR
WDIR=..

include ../prod/RULES.mi
include ../prod/MAKE.mi

CNAME=maint
IDIR=${IMAGE}/install
ODIR=${IMGDIR}/${OPTDIR}
FILES=${IDIR}/INSTALL ${IDIR}/UNINSTALL ${IDIR}/RUN
OPTION=${ODIR}/${PROD}.name
SRC=INSTALL.sh UNINSTALL.sh RUN.sh

build print clean rmbin::
        @echo "Starting to $@ ${CNAME}"
```

```
build:: ${FILES} ${OPTION}

print:: prtdate

clean::
        -rm -f prtdate

rmbin::
        -rm -f ${FILES} ${OPTION}

build print clean rmbin::
        @echo "Finished $@ of ${CNAME}"

.DEFAULT:
        @echo "No $@ procedure for the ${CNAME} component"

${FILES}: $$(@F).sh ${INCSFM}/sh_m4def.m4 ${INCSFM}/sh_stdhdr.m4
include ../prod/M4SHDR.mi
                -DINC="${INCSFM}" -D${BLDMAC} \
                ${INCSFM}/sh_m4def.m4 ${@F}.sh > $@
        chmod ug+x $@

${OPTION}: menu.txt
        ${M4} menu.txt >$@
        chmod 664 $@

include ../prod/PRINT.mi
```

Notes to Maintenance Makefile

1. Since the scripts in this component are only to be executed when installing the software package from a floppy disk, they are not installed on the local machine. Hence, there is no need for an install target.

2. The menu.txt file is preprocessed by the **m4** command to remove the SCCS ID information.

File Name: INSTALL.sh

```
:
ifdef(~INC~,,~define(INC,/usr/local/include)~)dnl
minclude(INC/sh_stdhdr.m4)dnl
# %W% %F% %Y% %D% %Q%

# INSTALL - Install Software Package from Mountable Device
```

```
USAGE="usage: INSTALL {device driver} {mount directory} {device name}"

# Exit codes and their meanings
# 0 - Normal
# 1 - Error

ERET1=1

# Temporary file definitions
TMP1=/usr/tmp/$$dt1

# Variable definitions
DEFGRP=bin
DEFOWN=bin
EVAL=eval 1> /dev/null 2>&1
PATH=/bin:/usr/bin:/etc

# Interrupt trap
trap "rm -f /usr/tmp/$$*" 0 1 2 3 15

# Save the input parameters

DDRIVE=${1:-/dev/SA}
IDIR=${2:-/install}
NDRIVE=${3:-diskette}

# Display Software Package Information
# Assumes presence of standard what string header
# which will be affixed when the script is processed
# by make (see sfmhdr.sh in ../common).

tput clear; echo
what $0 | sed -n '2,5p'
echo '\n'

# Get names of Owner and Group IDs

echo "\
** Owner and Group IDs **
To separate installed packages from standard
UNIX, it is suggested that the programs and directories
be given different Owner and Group IDs. For example,
the Owner could be \"local\" and the Group could be \"local\".
If no name is entered, the programs and directories will
be installed as Owner=$DEFOWN and Group=$DEFGRP.\n"

while true
```

```
do
  echo "Enter Owner ID (default=$DEFOWN): \c"
  read NEWOWN
  grep "^${NEWOWN:=$DEFOWN}" /etc/passwd > /dev/null && break
  echo "Invalid Owner Id"
done

while true
do
  echo "Enter Group ID (default=$DEFGRP): \c"
  read NEWGRP
  grep "^${NEWGRP:=$DEFGRP}" /etc/group > /dev/null && break
  echo "Invalid Group Id"
done

# Build file list
cd $IDIR
if $EVAL "(find usr/sfm -depth -print 1> $TMP1 &&
          find usr/linclude -type f -print 1>> $TMP1 &&
          find usr/llib -type f -print 1>> $TMP1 &&
          find usr/lshlib -type f -print 1>> $TMP1 &&
          find usr/admin/menu/packagemgmt/sfmmgmt -depth \
              -print 1>> $TMP1 &&
          find usr/options -type f -print 1>> $TMP1)"
then
  true
else
  echo "Error trying to read $NDRIVE"
  exit $ERET1
fi

# Copy files from floppy to proper directory
echo "Copying files\c"
if $EVAL "(cat $TMP1 | cpio -pdlm / 2>/dev/null)"
then
  echo " - completed"
else
  echo " - failed"
  exit $ERET1
fi

# Change Owner and Group IDs
echo "Changing Owner and Group IDs\c"
cd /
if $EVAL "(cat $TMP1 | xargs chown $NEWOWN &&
          cat $TMP1 | xargs chgrp $NEWGRP)"
then
  echo " - completed"
```

```
else
  echo " - failed"
  exit $ERET1
fi

# update executable files to show date installed
mcs -a "@(#)Installed on `date '+%D at %T'`." 1> /dev/null 2>&1 \
        /usr/sfm/sfintxx /usr/llib/libsfm.a \
        /usr/llib/libsfm_s.a /usr/lshlib/libsfm_s

echo "\
Install of Source File Management Tools completed.

This package is based on the concepts defined in Software Management under
UNIX by Israel Silverberg. After setting up a package according to the
requirements set forth in this book, you will need to create a copy of the
SCCS interface program for the package. This can be done through the Pack-
age Management Menu."
```

Notes to INSTALL.sh

1. The **ifdef** macro line shows how to define a default definition for the **m4** command. As with all shell scripts, the standard package header is incorporated via the two include files (sh_m4def.m4 and sh_stdhdr.sh).

2. By suffixing each command with the dnl macro, it is possible to prevent the blank lines that would be produced by these statements from being sent to standard output.

3. This shell script has been designed to be executed via the **sysadm** command or as a stand-alone shell script.

4. Every directory and file that is part of the software package will have the owner ID and group ID changed. However, directories that are not part of the software package will not be altered. The distinction is maintained by using the *-depth* option of the **find** command for the first case and the *-type f* option for the second.

5. The **mcs** command is used to update the comments section of the object files that contains a *.comment* section.

File Name: UNINSTALL.sh

```
:
ifdef(~INC~,,~define(INC,/usr/local/include)~)dnl
minclude(INC/sh_stdhdr.m4)dnl
# %W% %F% %Y% %D% %Q%
```

```
# UNINSTALL - Remove Installed Package from Machine

USAGE="usage: UNINSTALL {device driver} {mount directory} {device name}"

# Exit codes and their meanings
# 0 - Normal
# 1 - Error

ERET1=1

# Temporary file definitions
TMP1=/usr/tmp/$$dt1

# Variable definitions
EVAL=eval 1> /dev/null 2>&1
PATH=/bin:/usr/bin:/etc

# Interrupt trap
trap "rm -f /usr/tmp/$$*" 0 1 2 3 15

# Save the input parameters

DDRIVE=${1:-/dev/SA}
IDIR=${2:-/install}
NDRIVE=${3:-diskette}

# Display Software Package Information
# Assumes presence of standard what string header,
# which will be affixed when the script is processed
# by make (see sfmhdr.sh in ../common).

tput clear; echo
what $0 | sed -n '2,5p'
echo '\n'

# Verify that the package is to be removed

while true
do
  echo "Are you sure you wish to remove this package (y or n): \c"
  read ANS
  case "$ANS" in
    y|Y) break;;
    n|N) exit;;
    *)   echo "Invalid Answer";;
  esac
done
# Remove files from system
```

```
echo "Removing files\c"
cd $IDIR
if $EVAL "(find usr/sfm -type f -print 1> $TMP1 &&
          find usr/linclude -type f -print 1>> $TMP1 &&
          find usr/llib -type f -print 1>> $TMP1 &&
          find usr/lshlib -type f -print 1>> $TMP1 &&
      find usr/admin/menu/packagemgmt/sfmmgmt -type f -print 1>> $TMP1 &&
          find usr/options -type f -print 1>> $TMP1)"
then
  cd /
  if $EVAL "(cat $TMP1 | xargs rm -f)"
  then
    echo " - completed"
  else
    echo " - error in removing files"
    exit $ERET1
  fi
else
  echo " - error trying to read $NDRIVE"
  exit $ERET1
fi

# Attempt to remove directories related to package
echo "Removing package related directories\c"
cd $IDIR
if $EVAL "(find usr/sfm -type d -print 1> $TMP1 &&
  find /usr/admin/menu/packagemgmt/sfmmgmt -type d -print 1>> $TMP1)"
then
  cd /
  for i in `cat $TMP1 | xargs`
  do
    if $EVAL "rmdir $i 2>/dev/null"
    then
      true
    else
      echo " - error removing $i. Please check."
      echo "Continuing\c"
    fi
  done
else
  echo " - error trying to read $NDRIVE"
  exit $ERET1
fi
echo " - finished removing directories"

echo "Removal of Source File Management Tools completed."
```

Notes to UNINSTALL.sh

1. To prevent accidental deletion of a software package, every UNINSTALL script must check to see if the user really wants to delete the package.

2. Only the files that are present on the distribution disk will be deleted and only empty directories related to the software package are removed. To upgrade to a new version, the old package is deleted and the new package is installed. If the user has any special files, they will not be disturbed.

File Name: RUN.sh

```
:
ifdef(~INC~,,~define(INC,/usr/local/include)~)dnl
minclude(INC/sh_stdhdr.m4)dnl
# %W% %F% %Y% %D% %Q%

# RUN - Run Software Package from Mountable Device

USAGE="usage: RUN {device driver} {mount directory} {device name}"

# Exit codes and their meanings
# 0 - Normal
# 1 - Error

ERET1=1

# Variable definitions
PATH=/bin:/usr/bin:/etc

# Interrupt trap
trap "rm -f /usr/tmp/$$*" 0 1 2 3 15

# Save the input parameters

DDRIVE=${1:-/dev/SA}
IDIR=${2:-/install}
NDRIVE=${3:-diskette}

# Display Software Package Information
# Assumes presence of standard what string header,
# which will be affixed when the script is processed
# by make (see sfmhdr.sh in ../common).

tput clear; echo
```

```
what $0 | sed -n '2,5p'
echo '\n'

# Display message about software package

echo "\
This package is not executable from the floppy disk.
It must be installed and then sfintxx must be copied
to each package name for which it is to be used. For
example, the following would create the interface to
a package called \"gl\":
        cp sfintxx sfintgl
        chown gl sfintgl
        chgrp gl sfintgl
        chmod 4710 sfintgl
        ln sfintgl cdcgl

For more information, see Source File Managment with
SCCS by Israel Silverberg.\n"

echo "Press the any key to return\c"
read ANS
```

Notes to RUN.sh

The purpose of the shell script is to allow the software package to be executed from the
distribution media. Although the package we are building does not lend itself to execution
from the distribution media, a RUN script is still necessary for proper execution of the
sysadm command. In the preceding case, we use this option to provide information about
the package.

File Name: menu.txt

```
dnl Menu Description for Software Management Menu
dnl %W% %F% %Y% %D% %Q%
Source File Management Package
```

Notes to menu.txt

1. The first two lines are used merely to describe the source file and will be removed
   when processed by the **m4** command.

Management Component: "pkgmgmt"

Component

pkgmgmt

Description

The package management makefile builds and installs the Package Management package objects, which interface to the **sysadm** command. The action targets are as follows:

build   Build component and place objects in image directory.

install   Install package objects on local machine.

mktool   Not implemented at component level.

mkprod   Not implemented at component level.

print   Print the source files that have changed since the last execution of this target.

lint   Not implemented for this component.

clean   Remove extraneous work files.

rmbin   Remove objects from image directory.

load   Not implemented at component level.

save   Not implemented at component level.

The default is to execute the **build** target.

Examples

$ make
$ make build

Files

Besides the component makefile, this component contains all the shell scripts that are necessary to support the *Package Management Option* of the **sysadm** command. These scripts are as follows:

  DESC.sh, addprod.sh, delprod.sh

Source

All the source files for this component are listed in this appendix.

File Name: Makefile

```
#   Component Makefile for Source File Management Tools
#
#   Component: pkgmgmt
#
#   %W% %F% %Y% %D% %Q%
#

# Default definition for WDIR
WDIR=..

include ../prod/RULES.mi
include ../prod/MAKE.mi

CNAME=pkgmgmt
IDIR=${IMGDIR}/${PKGDIR}
PDIR=${INSDIR}/${PKGDIR}
FILES=${IDIR}/DESC ${IDIR}/addprod ${IDIR}/delprod
INSTF=${PDIR}/DESC ${PDIR}/addprod ${PDIR}/delprod
SRC=DESC.sh addprod.sh delprod.sh

build install print clean rmbin::
        @echo "Starting to $@ ${CNAME}"

build:: ${FILES}

install:: ${INSTF}
```

```
print:: prtdate

clean::
        -rm -f prtdate

rmbin::
        -rm -f ${FILES}

build install print clean rmbin::
        @echo "Finished $@ of ${CNAME}"

.DEFAULT:
        @echo "No $@ procedure for the ${CNAME} component"

${FILES}: $$(@F).sh ${INCSFM}/sh_m4def.m4 ${INCSFM}/sh_stdhdr.m4
include ../prod/M4SHDR.mi
                -DINC=${INCSFM} -D${BLDMAC} \
                ${INCSFM}/sh_m4def.m4 ${@F}.sh > $@
        chmod 640 $@

${INSTF}: ${IDIR}/$$(@F)
        ${INSTALL} -f ${@D} -m 640 -u ${OWNER} -g ${GROUP} ${IDIR}/${@F}

include ../prod/PRINT.mi
```

Notes to Package Management Makefile

1. This makefile is a good model for a component consisting of shell scripts: it is simple, it is not concerned with any special conditions and, above all, it is short.

File Name: DESC.sh

```
:
ifdef(~INC~,,~define(INC,/usr/local/include)~)dnl
minclude(INC/sh_stdhdr.m4)dnl
#ident "%W% %F% %Y% %D% %Q%"
#head#                         SOURCE FILE MANAGEMENT
#menu# software management menu
#help#
#help# This menu allows one to create a new interface program
#help# or to delete an existing program. The User ID and
#help# Group ID for the interface program must exist.
```

Notes to DESC.sh

1. This is the menu description file for the directory whose name is used as a menu option by the **sysadm** command.

2. The #menu# line is the menu description entry for the Package Management Menu.

3. The #help# lines constitute the help message for the preceding menu option.

4. The #head# line will be used as the menu header for the menu to be created if this option is chosen.

File Name: addprod.sh

```
:
ifdef(~INC~,,~define(INC,/usr/local/include)~)dnl
minclude(INC/sh_stdhdr.m4)dnl
#ident "%W% %F% %Y% %D% %Q%"
#menu# add package to source file management
#help#
#help# Before a package can be accessed using the source file
#help# tools, it must have an interface program. This routine
#help# establishes an interface program and sets the user ID and
#help# group ID. However, the package still must be set up
#help# in the correct format in the Source Library.

flags="-q q -k $$"
SFMDIR="/usr/sfm"

trap exit 1 2 15
trap '  trap "" 1 2 15
        rm -f /tmp/$$*' 0

while true
do
   echo "Enter Package ID or return to exit: \c"
   read PID
   if [ -z "$PID" ]
   then
     exit
   fi
   if [ -f $SFMDIR/sfint$PID ]
   then
     echo '\
The interface program for this package already exits.'
```

```
      continue
   fi
   break
done

while true
do
   echo "Enter Owner ID: \c"
   read OWNID
   grep "$OWNID" /etc/passwd > /dev/null && break
   echo "Invalid Owner ID"
done

while true
do
   echo "Enter Group ID: \c"
   read GRPID
   grep "$GRPID" /etc/passwd > /dev/null && break
   echo "Invalid Group ID"
done

cp $SFMDIR/sfintxx $SFMDIR/sfint$PID
chown $OWNID $SFMDIR/sfint$PID
chgrp $GRPID $SFMDIR/sfint$PID
chmod 4710 $SFMDIR/sfint$PID
ln $SFMDIR/sfint$PID $SFMDIR/cdc$PID

echo "Interface program for $PID has been created."
```

Notes to addprod.sh

1. What identifies this shell script as a menu entry is the #menu# line, which is the menu description entry for the submenu defined by this directory.

2. The #help# lines define the help message for this shell script.

3. The remainder of the shell script performs the action specified by the menu option.

4. This particular shell script is used to create an SCCS interface program from the sfintxx program. The "xx" is replaced by a proper package name, and the owner and group IDs are defined.

File Name: delprod.sh

```
:
ifdef(~INC~,,~define(INC,/usr/local/include)~)dnl
minclude(INC/sh_stdhdr.m4)dnl
#ident "%W% %F% %Y% %D% %Q%"
#menu# delete source file interface program
#help#
#help# Deletes the special interface program for a package from
#help# the source file management directory.

flags="-q q -k $$"
SFMDIR=/usr/sfm

trap exit 1 2 15
trap '  trap "" 1 2 15
        rm -f /tmp/$$*' 0

while true
do
  echo "Enter Package ID or return to exit: \c"
  read PID
  if [ -z "$PID" ]
  then
    exit
  fi
  if [ ! -f $SFMDIR/sfint$PID ]
  then
    echo "Interface program for $PID not found."
    continue
  fi
  break
done

while true
do
  echo "Are you sure you want to delete the Interface for $PID: \c"
  read ANS
  case "$ANS" in
    y|Y) break;;
    n|N) exit;;
    *)   echo "Invalid Answer";;
  esac
done

rm -f $SFMDIR/sfint$PID
rm -f $SFMDIR/cdc$PID
echo "Interface program for $PID removed."
```

Notes to delprod.sh

1. Notes 1 through 3 for addprod.sh also apply to this script.

2. This script is used to delete the SCCS interface program for a particular software package.

APPENDIX G

Scripts Component: "scripts"

Component

scripts

Description

The scripts makefile builds and installs all the source file management shell scripts for the software package. The action targets are as follows:

build	Build component and place objects in image directory.
install	Install package objects on local machine.
mktool	Not implemented at component level.
mkprod	Not implemented at component level.
print	Print the source files that have changed since the last execution of this target.
lint	Not implemented for this component.
clean	Remove extraneous work files.
rmbin	Remove objects from image directory.
load	Not implemented at component level.
save	Not implemented at component level.

The default is to execute the **build** target.

Examples

$ make
$ make build

Files

Besides the component makefile, this component contains all the shell scripts described in Appendixes D and F of Silverberg, *Source File Management with SCCS.*

Source

Only the source for the makefile is provided in this appendix. The following changes have been made to the shell scripts to implement the concepts presented in this work:

1. "getst.sh" and "sget.sh" needed to be modified to support the use of the delta time stamp as described in Section 6.4.2.

2. All of the shell scripts need to be changed to support the revised package header. The change consists of adding the following two lines after the first line:

   :
   ifdef(~INC~,,~define(INC,/usr/local/include)~)dnl
   minclude(INC/sh_stdhdr.m4)dnl

File Name: Makefile

```
#   Component Makefile for Source File Management Tools
#
#   Component: scripts
#
#   %W% %F% %Y% %D% %Q%
#

# Default definition for WDIR
WDIR=..

include ../prod/RULES.mi
include ../prod/MAKE.mi

CNAME=scripts
IDIR=${IMGDIR}/${SFMDIR}
PDIR=${INSDIR}/${SFMDIR}
FILES=${IDIR}/deltast ${IDIR}/dted ${IDIR}/getst ${IDIR}/mrval \
```

```
        ${IDIR}/pvinit ${IDIR}/sdelta ${IDIR}/setsfm ${IDIR}/sfinit \
        ${IDIR}/sget ${IDIR}/srmdel ${IDIR}/sunget ${IDIR}/verst
INSTF=${PDIR}/deltast ${PDIR}/dted ${PDIR}/getst ${PDIR}/mrval \
        ${PDIR}/pvinit ${PDIR}/sdelta ${PDIR}/setsfm ${PDIR}/sfinit \
        ${PDIR}/sget ${PDIR}/srmdel ${PDIR}/sunget ${PDIR}/verst
SRC=deltast.sh dted.sh getst.sh mrval.sh pvinit.sh sdelta.sh setsfm.sh \
        sfinit.sh sget.sh srmdel.sh sunget.sh verst.sh


build install print clean rmbin::
        @echo "Starting to $@ ${CNAME}"


build:: ${FILES}


install:: ${INSTF}


print:: prtdate


clean::
        -rm -f prtdate


rmbin::
        -rm -f ${FILES}


build install print clean rmbin::
        @echo "Finished $@ of ${CNAME}"


.DEFAULT:
        @echo "No $@ procedure for the ${CNAME} component"


${FILES}: $$(@F).sh ${INCSFM}/sh_m4def.m4 ${INCSFM}/sh_stdhdr.m4
include ../prod/M4SHDR.mi
                -DINC=${INCSFM} -D${BLDMAC} \
                ${INCSFM}/sh_m4def.m4 ${@F}.sh > $@
        chmod +x $@


${INSTF}: ${IDIR}/$$(@F)
        ${INSTALL} -f ${@D} -m 755 -u ${OWNER} -g ${GROUP} ${IDIR}/${@F}


include ../ptof/zptiny.mi
```

Notes to Scripts Makefile

Except for the longer list of files to be built and installed, this shell script is the same as the one shown in Appendix F. The advantage of boiler-plate shell scripts is that they can be implemented in most components with a minimum number of changes.

SCCS Interface Component: "sfint"

Component

sfint

Description

The SCCS interface makefile controls all actions involved in the building and installing of the SCCS interface program. The action targets are as follows:

build   Build component and place objects in image directory.

install   Install package objects on local machine.

mktool   Not implemented at component level.

mkprod   Not implemented at component level.

print   Print the source files that have changed since the last execution of this target.

lint   Check C source files with lint.

clean   Remove extraneous work files.

rmbin   Remove objects from image directory.

load   Not implemented at component level.

save   Not implemented at component level.

The default is to execute the **build** target.

Examples

$ make
$ make clean

Files

Besides the component makefile, the only other file is the C source file for the SCCS inter-face program, sfintxx.c. The file has been modified to support both the archive and shared libraries defined in Chapter 11.

Source

All the source files for this component are listed in this appendix.

File Name: Makefile

```
#   Component Makefile for Source File Management Tools
#
#   Component: sfint
#
#   %W% %F% %Y% %D% %Q%
#

# Default definition for WDIR
WDIR=..

include ../prod/RULES.mi
include ../prod/MAKE.mi

CNAME=sfint
IDIR=${IMGDIR}/${SFMDIR}
PDIR=${INSDIR}/${SFMDIR}
FILES=${IDIR}/sfintxx
INSTF=${PDIR}/sfintxx
SRC=sfintxx.c
LINTF=${SRC:.c=.ln}

build install lint print clean rmbin::
        @echo "Starting to $@ ${CNAME}"

build:: ${FILES}

install:: ${INSTF}
```

```
lint:: ${INCSFM}/c_stdhdr.m4
include ../prod/M4SHDR.mi
            ${INCSFM}/c_stdhdr.m4 > c_stdhdr.h

lint:: ${LINTF} ${LIBSFM}/libsfm.a ${INCSFM}/libsfm.h
        ${LINT} ${LTFLAGS} -D${MACHINE} -D${BLDMAC} -I${INCSFM} \
            -L ${LIBSFM} -lsfm ${LINTF}


print:: prtdate

clean::
        -rm -f *.o *.ln prtdate c_stdhdr.h

rmbin::
        -rm -f ${FILES}

build install lint print clean rmbin::
        @echo "Finished $@ of ${CNAME}"

.DEFAULT:
        @echo "No $@ procedure for the ${CNAME} component"

${IDIR}/sfintxx: $$(@F).c ${INCSFM}/c_stdhdr.m4 ${LIBSFM}/libsfm.a \
            ${LIBSFM}/libsfm_s.a ${INCSFM}/libsfm.h
include ../prod/M4SHDR.mi
            ${INCSFM}/c_stdhdr.m4 > c_stdhdr.h
        ${CC} ${CFLAGS} ${CTOOLS} -D${MACHINE} -D${BLDMAC} -I${INCSFM} \
            ${@F}.c -L ${LIBSFM} -lsfm_s -lsfm ${SHLIB} -o $@
        chmod 600 $@
        rm c_stdhdr.h

${INSTF}: ${IDIR}/$$(@F)
        ${INSTALL} -f ${@D} -m 600 -u ${OWNER} -g ${GROUP} ${IDIR}/${@F}
        ${STRIP} ${STRPFLG} $@
        ${MCS} -d -a "@(#)Installed on `date '+%D at %T'`." $@

include ../prod/PRINT.mi
```

Notes to SCCS Interface Makefile

1. This makefile can be used as a model for any makefile that compiles a C program. It shows how to interface with include files, archive libraries, shared libraries, and lint libraries that are part of the package.

2. Because of the package header include file, the lint make rule is divided into two
   parts. The first part builds the necessary include file and the second part runs lint
   on the source file. Although it is not a documented option, the **-L** option on the

lint command line is recognized by **lint**. Here, we are using it to point to the lint library created by the library component.

3. The dependency line for sfintxx links the building of sfintxx to any library change, rather than being linked to individual members. This more general approach resolves the problem of what happens if an object module called by the member changes, but the member object module itself does not change.

4. The package header file (c_stdhdr.m4) is first processed by **m4**, which creates a normal C include file. This is done to circumvent the string substitution limitation of **cpp**.

5. When the program is installed, the symbol table and debugging information are no longer needed. The **strip** command in the "install" make rule removes this information. The **mcs** command adds an installation message to the *.comment* section.

File Name: sfintxx.c

```
/* sfint.c - SCCS Command Interface Program */

/* performs a setuid and setgid to the owner
   and group IDs of this program. This program
   provides an interface for the get, delta, unget
   rmdel, cdc, and the "admin -t" commands.
*/

#ident "%W% %F% %Y% %D% %Q%"

#include <stdio.h>
#include <sys/types.h>
#include <string.h>
#include <libsfm.h>
#include "c_stdhdr.h"

#define USAGE"\
usage: getxx [options] {SCCS File name}\n\
       deltaxx [options] {SCCS File name}\n\
       cdcxx [options] {SCCS File name}\n\
       rmdelxx -r{SID} {SCCS File name}\n\
       ungetxx [options] {SCCS File name}\n\
       where xx is the package name.\n"

#define ADMERR "ERROR: Only -t option allowed with admin\n"
#define NOSDIR "ERROR: Unknown SCCS Directory\n"
#define NOWDIR "ERROR: Unknown Work Directory\n"
#define NOCDIR "ERROR: Unknown Current Work Directory\n"
```

```c
#define ERET1 1
#define TRUE 1
#define FALSE 0
#define MAXCMD 7
#define PATHLEN 64

/* SCCS Command List */

char    *cdir = "/usr/bin/";
char    *vcmd[] = { "sfint", "get", "delta", "unget", "rmdel", \
                    "cdc", "admin" };
int     aflag = FALSE;

/* Variable Definition */

char    **nargv;
void    appath(), exit(), perror();

main(argc, argv, envp)
int     argc;
char    **argv, **envp;
{
        int     i, j;
        char    *path;
        char    tmp1[PATHLEN];
        nargv = (char **)calloc((unsigned)argc, sizeof (char **));

        if (argc < 2 || (i = chkcmd(argc, argv)) == 0) {
                fprintf(stderr,USAGE);
                exit (ERET1);
        }
        nargv[0] = vcmd[i];
        strcat((path = cdir), vcmd[i]);
        if (strcmp(vcmd[i], "admin") == 0) aflag = TRUE;
        j = 1;
        for (i = 1; i < argc; i++) {
                if (*argv[i] == '-') switch (argv[i][1]) {
                case 'C':
                        continue;
                  case 't':
                        nargv[j++] = argv[i];
                        continue;
                default :
                        if (aflag == TRUE) {
                                fprintf(stderr,ADMERR);
                                exit (ERET1);
                        }
                        nargv[j++] = argv[i];
                        continue;
```

```
            }
            else if (*argv[i] == '/') nargv[j++] = argv[i];
            else if (*argv[i] != '\0') {
                    strcpy(tmp1, argv[i]);
                    appath(tmp1);
                    nargv[j++] = tmp1;
            }
        }
        nargv[j] = NULL;
        execve(path, nargv, envp);
        fprintf(stderr, "ERROR: cannot execute %s", path);
        exit (ERET1);
}

/* Check for valid command */

int chkcmd(narg, targ)
int     narg;
char    **targ;
{
        int     i;
        char    *j, *tmpc;

        j = strrchr(targ[0], '\/');
        tmpc = (j == 0) ? targ[0] : ++j;
        if (strncmp(tmpc, "sfint", 5) == 0) {
                for (i = 1; i < narg; i++) {
                        if (*targ[i] == '-' && targ[i][1] == 'C')
                                tmpc = &targ[i][2];
                }
        }
        for (i = 1; i < MAXCMD; i++) {
                if (!strncmp(tmpc, vcmd[i], (strlen(vcmd[i]))))
                        return(i);
        }
        return(0);
}

/* Append SCCS and Component portions of path */

void appath(sfile)
char    *sfile;
{
        char    *getenv(), *getcwd(), *sdir, *wdir, *cwd;
        char    cmpnt[PATHLEN];
        char    tname[PATHLEN];
```

```
      if ((sdir = getenv("SDIR")) == NULL) {
            fprintf(stderr,NOSDIR);
            exit (ERET1);
      }
      if ((wdir = getenv("WDIR")) == NULL) {
            fprintf(stderr,NOWDIR);
            exit (ERET1);
      }
      if ((cwd = getenv("CDIR")) == NULL) {
            fprintf(stderr,NOCDIR);
            exit (ERET1);
      }
      (void)substr(cmpnt, cwd, (strlen(wdir)), (strlen(cwd)));
      sprintf(tname, "%s%s\/%s", sdir, cmpnt, sfile);
      strcpy(sfile, tname);
}
```

Notes to sfintxx.c

1. Except for the changes indicated next, this is the same source file as described in Appendix E of Silverberg, *Source File Management with SCCS*.

2. Instead of the package header being a separate object module linked to this object module, it is incorporated as an include file (c_stdhdr.h).

3. The "substr" function has been removed and used to show how to build libraries. To support this new library, the library include file (libsfm.h) is now included.

Glossary

Application package objects--Whether they are *package objects* for a general ledger or a compiler, application package objects are the set of objects that constitutes the reason for the existence of the *software package*.

Archive library--A collection of individual files placed into a single file. An archive library file may consist of object files, data files, source files, or any mixture of these.

Base name--A file name that has no suffix.

Build process--The collective transformation of the raw material (source files, data files, and instructions) into the *package objects* that form a *software package*.

Command line--When the *target* is out of date, the command lines associated with a *make rule* are executed. Each command line is treated as a separate shell script, with the environment being set by the **make** command.

Command line macro definition--A *macro definition line* that occurs on the **make** command line.

Common archive library--An *archive library* file that contains object modules shared by several *software packages*.

Component--A stand-alone building block that may be a *package object*, or used to build a package object, or both. A component may contain one or more subcomponents. As a part of a source tree, the directories immediately under the software package directory are components.

Component makefile--A *makefile* used to build a *compone*nt or subcomponent.

Configuration package objects--The set of *package objects* used to configure the environment of the *application package objects*.

Default macro definition--The term refers to the *macro names* defined in the *internal description file*.

Default make rules--The term refers to the *make rules* defined in the *internal description file*.

Dependency line--The dependency line defines the relationship between the *target* (the object to be built) and its dependencies, which may be files or other targets. If any dependency has a more recent modification time than the target, then the *command lines* are executed.

Dependency tree--The hierarchical structure resulting from the organization of the dependencies in the *dependency line* until the nodes are file names or null target names.

Description file--This is another name for a *makefile*.

Development machine--The machine on which the *work source tree* is located. It is also the machine on which the *software package* will be built.

Distributed archive library--An *archive library* file that is distributed with the *software package*.

Explicit macro definition--A *macro definition line* that occurs within a makefile is called an explicit macro definition.

Host shared library file--A *shared library* file used during the link edit phase that incorporates pointers to the *target shared library file* into the *package object*.

Inference rule--An inference rule is a special *make rule*. It is also known as a transformation rule since it defines the transformation of an object with one suffix to that with another suffix.

Inference target--The target name for an *inference rule* that has a special format defined as {from suffix}{to suffix}.

Internal description file--The **make** command has an internal description file to which the external makefiles are appended. This internal description file contains *macro definition lines*, *make rules*, and *inference rules*.

Internal macro--The **$@**, **$?**, **$%**, **$***, and **$<** are referred to as internal macros. Their definition is determined during the processing of the *makefile*.

Macro definition--A macro definition can be any string of characters, except a pound sign (**#**). The macro definition replaces the *macro name* when the macro name is prefixed by a dollar sign (**$**).

Macro definition line--A macro definition line associates a *macro name* with a *macro definition*. Should a macro name have multiple definitions, only the last macro definition applies. The macro name is not prefixed by a dollar sign (**$**) when it appears on the macro definition line.

Macro name--The macro name is any string of alphabetic or numeric characters that does not contain any one of the metacharacters (**$**, **@**, **#**, **=**, *****, **&**, **( )**, **{ }**, **<tab>**, or **<space>**). A macro name may or may not have an associated *macro definition*.

Maintenance package objects--The set of *package objects* used to install or remove a *software package*.

Make rule--A make rule consists of a *dependency line* plus optional *command lines*. The make rule tells the **make** command what action to take on the specified *target* or targets.

Makefile--The source file containing the *make rules* for the **make** command. The makefile is sometimes referred to as the *description file*.

Package archive library--An *archive library* file used only to build a *software package* and not counted as a *package object*.

Package image tree--The structure into which the output of the build process is placed. It is a mirror image of the target structure for the *software package*.

Package object--A package object may be an executable file, a data file, or the name of a directory. Each package object belongs to one of three sets: *application package objects*, *maintenance package objects*, *or configuration package objects*.

Product makefile--A *makefile* used to build a *software package*.

SCCS source tree--The source tree for a *software package*, which consists of *components*, *subcomponents*, and SCCS files.

Shared library--The shared library is based on the notion that more than one process can share common object modules during execution. A shared library is composed of a *host shared library file* and a *target shared library file*.

Software package--A software package consists of one or more sets of *package objects*. Every software package contains a set of package objects called the *application package objects*. Optionally, the software package may contain sets for *maintenance package objects* and *configuration package objects*.

Source library machine--The machine that contains the *SCCS source tree* for a *software package*.

Subcomponent--A *component*, such as an archive library, contains subcomponents for each object module in the library. Thus, a subcomponent has the same characteristics as a component. Just as a component is a buildable unit, a subcomponent is a buildable unit.

Target--For a *make rule*, the target is the object to be made by the make rule. A null target is valid and will always be treated as out of date.

Target machine--The machine on which the released *software package* is to be executed. The target machine is distinct from the *verification machine*, even though the software package is executed on both.

Target shared library--The *shared library* file used when a *package object* is executed. The object modules in the target shared library may be shared by more than one process.

Tools library--When version control of the software tools used to build a software package is needed, the software tools need to be stored in a tools library. The tools library has separate directories for each software tool package. Within each package, there is a separate directory for each version.

Verification machine--The machine on which the *software package* is verified or, in traditional terms, tested.

Work source tree--A mirror image of the *SCCS source tree* in which the SCCS files have been replaced by source files for a particular version of the *software package*.

Index

A

Action target, 94, 97, 169
Administrative targets, 97
Application makefile, 208, 210
Application package objects (*See* Package objects, application)
Archive library file, 16, 76–78, 147, 157, 186, 213, 217
    libsfm.h, 217
    substr.c, 189
ar command, 153, 156

B

Base name, 68, 217
Build instructions, 4, 6, 11, 12, 14, 17
Build process, 3, 6, 10, 11, 14, 127, 128, 133, 142, 156, 217
    make command, 16
    objectives, 12–14

C

cc command, 148
Command line, 16, 25–26, 32, 37, 41, 64, 217
    common, 56

D

T

Target, 16, 21–22, 220

Target machine, 10, 96, 144, 220

Target name, 22, 23, 37, 41, 42, 70, 77 *(See also* Special target names and Standard target names)

    concatenation, 57

Target path, 10, 11

Target shared library, 154, 156, 157, 186, 220

Text replacement, 126

    cpp, 128

    m4, 133

    vc, 139

Tools library, 101, 104, 175, 220

touch command, 95

Trojan horse, 104

tsort command, 153

typedef statements, 151

V

Variable name, 30, 37

vc command, 128, 138–40

Verification machine, 10, 220

Verification path, 10, 11

W

what strings, 145, 153, 175

Z

Zero defect software, 14